Mind Your Manners

Culture Clash in the
European Single Market

Mind Your Manners
JOHN MOLE

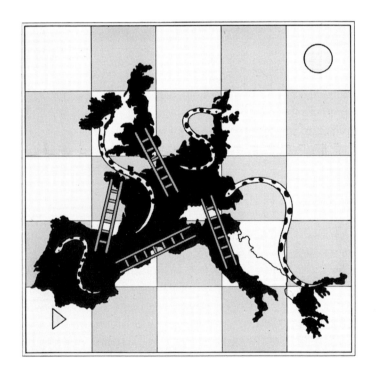

The Industrial Society

First published in 1990 by
The Industrial Society
Robert Hyde House
48 Bryanston Square
London W1H 7LN
Telephone 071 262 2401

ISBN 0 85290 469 – X

British Library Cataloguing in Publication Data
Mole, John
   Mind your manners : Managers guide to working in the
   single European market.
   1. European community. Countries. Etiquette in business.
   I. Title
   395.52094

Cover design by Philippa Bramson
Typeset by Columns of Reading
Printed and bound in Great Britain by
Biddles Limited, Guildford, Surrey

For Olivia
who defies stereotyping

CONTENTS

FOREWORD

As a regular traveller within Europe, on business and pleasure, I am most certainly aware of the need for this new publication.

Like many others, I suspect there have been times when I have misunderstood or misinterpreted business or social behaviour but have been forgiven by my hosts on the basis that I was an ignorant foreigner who did not know how to behave. How much better it would have been to have had that understanding and not make the mistake in the first place.

Within the European Single Market, working with other European managers will be increasingly common. It is crucial that we should be able to create effective working relationships rapidly. For all of us trying to work within this environment *Mind Your Manners'* unique approach will be of great value.

The book is a readable, entertaining and practical guide for the manager in Europe. It identifies areas of cross-cultural sensitivity within the organisational, legal, social and behavioural environments of business culture. It also complements The Industrial Society's management training activities in Europe.

Eric Molyneux
Division Director

ACKNOWLEDGEMENTS

Cross-national surveys provide useful data to help modify national stereotypes. I have quoted from the regular series of *Eurobarometer: public opinion in the European Community*, published by the European Commission, and from *British Social Attitudes Special International Report* published by Gower, 1989.

Many of the international accounting firms publish technical descriptions of business and accounting practice. The *Doing Business In* . . . series, published by Ernst and Whinney, is concise and lucid. For a broader but no less authoritative overview for the business traveller, the Economist Guides to a select number of countries including France, Germany, Italy and the United Kingdom are full of useful insights and information.

The academic study of international cultural difference is a fast-growing tributary of the mainstream of management science. It brings to the classic texts of organisational theory a wider perspective drawn from comparative studies in every branch of the humanities. The potential reading list is therefore vast. The following is a selection of those which most influenced the ideas in the second part of this book.

Adler, N. *International Dimensions of Organisational Behaviour* Kent: Kent Publishing Company, 1986

Basile, J. *La Formation Cuturelle des Cadres et des Dirigeants* Paris: Seghers, 1979

Gauthey, Ratiu, Rodgers, Xardel *Leaders sans Frontières* Paris: McGraw Hill, 1988

Hofstede, G. 'The cultural relativity of organisational practices and theories', *Journal of International Business Studies* February 1983

Hofstede, G. *Culture's Consequences* Beverly Hills: Sage, 1980

Inzerilli, G., and Laurent, A. 'Managerial views of organisation structure in France the the USA', *International Studies of Management and Organisation*, Vol XIII 1 and 2, M. E. Sharp Inc, 1983

Laurent, A. 'The cultural diversity of western conceptions of management', *International Studies of Management and Organisation* Vol XIII 1 and 2, M. E. Sharp Inc, 1983

Pascale and Athos *The Art Of Japanese Management* New York: Simon and Schuster, 1981

Schneider, S. *Strategy formulation, the impact of national cultures*, Working paper 87/38, Fontainebleau: INSEAD, 1987

Weinshall, T. D. *Culture and Management Penguin* London: 1977

Zimmerman, *Dealing with the Japanese* London: George Allen and Unwin, 1985

There are a growing number of consultants specialising in the field. Particularly helpful were Irene Rodgers of Intercultural Management Associates in Paris, Fons Trompenaars of the Centre for International Business Studies in Amsterdam, David Wheatley of Employment Conditions Abroad in London and Sue Davison of Pipal International in Oxford.

I am grateful to Jonathan Nevitt, Tristam and Katrin Carrington-Windo, Kate Icke, Graham Dodge, Katrin Kohl, Joan Gallagher, Michael Lucey and Sue Webb for reading parts of the manuscript and suggesting amendments. The errors and omissions and distortions which remain are all mine. Gilles Desmons and June Thompson at the Industrial Society were extremely supportive and tolerant.

Especially helpful with further introductions and practical

help were Mario Venturi, Panaghis Cavadias and Charles Burdett.

By far the biggest debt of gratitude is owed to all those who gave up their time so generously to share their experience and insights. I was very aware that while I was working they were not. Many of them are fellow graduates of INSEAD, itself a model of cross-cultural excellence.

INTRODUCTION

This book attempts to answer the following question:

'What do I need to know about colleagues from European Community countries that will help us work successfully together?'

The Single Market is bringing about an increasing number of joint ventures, mergers and acquisitions among European, American and Japanese companies. It is also prompting multinationals to convert national subsidiaries into product groups managed by multinational teams. Their effectiveness will depend on how well the managers of different nationalities work together.

Working together in the same organisation is different from doing business together as buyer and seller. It requires a deeper understanding of why people from different backgrounds behave the way they do.

A frequent reaction to the different ways that other people do things is judgemental and condescending — 'typical German/Italian/Brit' — or something much ruder. Our reactions derive as much from our own attitudes and values as from those underlying the behaviour of others. If this book is an encouragement to suspend judgement and ask why we react in the way we do, it will have succeeded.

There are two parts. The first consists of brief and generalised portraits of the countries of the EC, concentrating on aspects which most affect the national way of doing business. It provides the overall context in which individual organisations operate. It would be extraordinarily ambitious to attempt a comprehensive analysis of the business environment of twelve different countries. These chapters should be read in addition to more technical books on business practice, taxation, legislation, accounting and so on, as well as more general guides.

The second part goes deeper into the fundamental differences between European business cultures from the point of view of individual managers working within them. It looks at the attitudes, values and beliefs that have most influence on our working relationships with colleagues, bosses, subordinates and the outside world. It suggests a simple tool, the MOLE Map, for examining different ways in which organisations work.

While I am indebted to the academic works referred to in the acknowledgements, the principal source is informal interviews with almost 200 practicing managers, most of them expatriates. The principle was to talk to people of at least three different nationalities about each country. The result is therefore an amalgam of different national viewpoints.

THE SINGLE MARKET

The country sections that follow concentrate on those aspects of the business environment which were repeatedly mentioned in the interviews as important to an understanding of how business is conducted. They consist of generalisations collated from a number of sources which may not hold true in individual circumstances. Readers are advised to test them against their personal experience.

Six countries are dealt with more fully than the others because of the size of their markets and the number of companies involved in cross-border relationships: France, Germany, Italy, Netherlands, Spain and the United Kingdom. Readers are more likely to be involved with companies from these countries than from the others. (*See* the tables at the end of this chapter.) Some general observations can be made about all twelve countries.

Language

Almost everyone interviewed recommended that anyone embarking on a cross-border relationship should learn the language, including those interviews given by people working in Denmark and the Netherlands. Even if the initial contacts speak a second language you soon have to deal with those who do not. A recent survey asking people in how many languages they can follow a simple conversation, showed that except for Denmark, Luxembourg and the Netherlands the majority understand only their own language.

The EC has nine official languages. Several countries are multilingual. About 50 million of the EC population are estimated to be minority language speakers. While an ignorance of Frisian may not be a major stumbling block, a smattering of Flemish or Catalan will go a long way in Antwerp and Barcelona. Spanish is only the second language for a quarter of the population of Spain. Over 90 per cent of Italians speak a language or dialect in addition to the Tuscan version known as Italian. This is irrelevant if you are dealing only with senior managers but if you have bought a factory or are looking for local agents it might help to make at least a gesture towards the local language.

Regionalism

Gallia est omnis divisa in partes tres.

Julius Caesar

It is conventional for guides to begin by pointing out that countries are not homogeneous entities. This book is no exception. It is a paradox that as the European Community grows in strength so do regions. Some of them actively look to Brussels to help them foster their independence as national sovereignty diminishes.

Cultural, geographical and historical differences between regions are obvious and important, particularly to their inhabitants. In some countries it is very hard to get people to relocate out of their home region. Even if they are willing to move account must be taken of local feeling. Posting a Francophone Belgian to Antwerp or a Basque to Seville may make both sides uncomfortable. On the level of personal relationships and social contact it is essential to be aware of regional pride, even if it is only a question of pandering to a conceit. But their significance should not be overestimated. While there is a difference between, say, Roman Catholic, beer drinking, extrovert, lederhosen-sporting Bavaria and pietist, sober, modest, thrifty, wine-drinking Swabia, a native of Stuttgart has more in common with a native of Munich than either has with a non-German. And in the context of business attitudes and behaviour the difference in the way that BMW and Mercedes are managed is negligible.

The generation gap

> ... especially since the rise of the Greens a large section of youth has vigorously contested what it sees as the greedy materialism and bourgeois conformism of its parents and elders.
>
> *The Economist Guide*, Germany

This is true but it is also a truism. It could have been written about any country and at any time in the last few thousand years. It often was. The marvel is not the generation gap but how soon the young cross it.

Today's generation gap is particularly noticeable in Southern Europe where the traditional authority systems of church and family are rapidly losing ground and the average age of the population is lower than in the ageing north. In predominantly Catholic countries like Spain and Italy and Ireland issues such as cohabitation, abortion, and divorce have become subjects of open debate and legislative change where only a few years ago they would have been taboo.

The generation gap in business is between those who have professional training and those who do not. Again this is more noticeable in the south. A generation of professional managers under 40 years of age, educated mainly in American business techniques and outlook, are challenging the old ways of doing things.

Women

For the most part throughout this book, for 'he' read 'he or she'. Unfortunately this is not very realistic, particularly in senior positions and among expatriate managers. In 1987 Euro-barometer published the results of a survey which asked people what they thought were the ideal roles of men and women in the family.

The results shed an interesting light on northern preconceptions about the values of southern Europeans. There is no apparent geographical or cultural pattern of discrimination. Germany is much more resistant to women working than neighbouring Denmark, for example. Greece and the Netherlands have identical views. The polarisation between the extremes is also interesting. Ireland is much more divided on the subject than, say, Spain.

Attitudes towards women, held by both sexes, derive mainly from their perceived role outside rather than inside the workplace. The major problems specific to women are common to all cultures — combining family and career, maternity leave, provision of child care facilities, the need to do better than equivalent men — and far outweigh the problems they have as women in different types of business culture.

In terms of organisation and leadership I found little anecdotal evidence of significant differences between men and women. Women behaved in the same way men did. Those who did well in companies did so for similar reasons as the men. In some countries they owed their first opportunity to family or political connections, in others to professional qualifications, and everywhere their advancement to competence and luck. I could find no evidence that women bring anything particularly female to the job. If they are good bosses, for example, it is in the same way that men are good.

Work ethic

Southern Europeans work to live and Northern Europeans live to work.

The Protestant work ethic is said to have been one of the vital elements in the development of capitalism. There is a persistent conviction among northern Europeans that southerners are lazy. The different work ethic is said by northerners to be a major cultural hurdle when northern companies head to the sun and the cheap labour of the south. The British Social Attitudes Special International Report (1989) shows how the difference in work ethic translates into reality. The average length of the working week, 1985–1986, among full-time workers, employees and self-employed, was 44.9 hours in Germany and 42.4 hours in Italy. So the difference between the Protestant and the Catholic work ethic is two and a half hours a week. The British worked 42 hours which either ruins the theory or makes them honorary Latins.

The figures do not take into account that Germans have more paid holiday than Italians or Britons. Including public holidays, Germans have an average of 39 days paid holiday a year to Britain's 33 and Italy's 34. So although Germans have longer working weeks they have fewer of them.

The further south you go the more unreliable the statistics in evaluating how hard people work. Italy has a black economy estimated as the equivalent of 30-40 per cent of the white economy. By definition this does not show up in statistics. In Germany it is around 10 per cent and in the UK about 15 per cent. In Latin countries there is a much larger proportion of people who have second jobs, made easier by a working day that starts and finishes earlier. Outside the main cities this may include running a smallholding, the labour and the fruits of which do not turn up in the statistics.

Observation and anecdotal evidence support the argument that people work as hard in the south as in the north. To claim that one race or culture works harder than another is a subjective value judgement. There are indeed measurable differences between the productive and the less productive economies but the underlying cause is not how hard people work but how effectively. The problem is one of management, not motivation.

Business ethics

The national stereotypes to be most wary of are those propagated by nations about themselves. They express aspiration more often than reality and are rarely held by outsiders. When I mentioned that I was in the middle of writing this book the first question many people asked was which was the most untrustworthy nationality to do business with. I always named the nationality of the questioner. It wasn't only a put-down but a statement about the subjectivity and relativity of business ethics. Those who sincerely believe that they are solely responsible for maintaining standards of fair play and probity in the international community are often shocked to discover that foreigners think they are shifty and unreliable.

Underlying social values differ from country to country. Attitudes to government, family, local community, employer and employee differ. Southern Europeans castigated by northerners for corruption in public life look with equal disapproval at the collapse of family loyalties in the north. They regard it as a duty to cheat the taxman and resent criticism by paragons of civic virtue who put their parents into old people's homes.

There are different degrees of belief as to what constitutes actual wrongdoing. What is illegal need not be unethical and vice versa. For example, the status of insider dealing is ambiguous in many countries. Lavish and tax-deductible business entertainment may be considered legitimate in the private sector but bribery in the public sector. Social security fraud among the poor may be more severely pursued and punished than major commercial fraud.

Values differ from country to country about personal and civic duty. Would you lie to the police to protect a friend accused of VAT evasion? Would you award a contract to your brother-in-law or the lowest bidder? Does the likelihood of being found out make a difference? These questions have different answers depending on the social environment. The distinctions between absolute moral codes and the likelihood of being found out, pangs of conscience and social embarrassment, are more blurred in some societies than in others.

In day-to-day dealings conventions of behaviour can be misinterpreted. Among many westerners there is a presumption of dishonesty about people from cultures in which it is impolite to look others in the eye. Among Europeans the handshake at the end of a negotiation can be interpreted by one side as a sign that the deal is struck and by the other as a polite leave taking. A major international court case pivoted on the meaning of a handshake at the end of a meeting.

Normal practice can engender mistrust. Delaying payment of invoices until the very last minute is standard practice among some treasury managers but seen as sharp practice by foreigners. Missed delivery dates may be a normal part of doing business in one environment and morally, as well as commercially, reprehensible in others.

The attitude to agreements differ. Some look to the spirit of an agreement rather than the letter and are offended when their partner refuses to re-negotiate the terms because circumstances have changed. That partner is equally scandalised because he or she believes that the other party is trying to cheat.

Faced with such diversity the best course is probably to reserve ethical judgement for one's own behaviour and suspend it when looking at others'.

Tables

Populations

	Population (millions)	Official GDP ($ billions)
Germany	62	655
Italy	57	352
UK	56	455
France	55	517
Spain	38	161
Netherlands	14	132
Belgium	10	80
Greece	10	35
Portugal	10	21
Denmark	5	56
Ireland	4	18
Luxembourg	0.3	3

Cross-border activity

In the 12 months to 30 September 1989 companies in the EC countries made a total of 1500 cross-border acquisitions worldwide of which 754 were within the EC. The UK made by far the largest number, followed by France.

In addition, 206 EC companies were bought by North American companies and 230 by companies from the rest of the world — 62 by Swedes, 62 by Swiss, 30 by Japanese, 28 by Finns and 48 by other nationalities.

So within the EC about 1200 companies were bought by investors outside the home country. In addition some 1000 EC companies were involved in corporate partnerships, for example joint ventures or strategic cross-shareholdings.

Acquisitions of EC companies
September 1988–September 1989

	Number of EC companies buying other EC companies	Number of EC companies bought by foreign companies
UK	315	293
France	180	219
Germany	71	180
Netherlands	55	108
Italy	33	116
Spain	15	121
Belgium	20	65
Ireland	43	23
Denmark	9	26
Portugal		11
Greece		NA
Luxembourg		NA
TOTAL	754	1190

Source: KPMG *Deal Watch*.

Percentage of people who can follow a conversation
in another language

Number of languages	0	1	2	3+
Belgium	50	22	18	9
Denmark	40	30	25	6
Germany	60	33	6	1
Greece	66	27	5	2
France	67	26	6	1
Ireland	80	17	3	—
Italy	76	19	5	1
Luxembourg	1	10	47	42
Netherlands	28	29	32	12
Portugal	76	14	8	2
Spain	68	26	5	1
UK	74	20	5	1

Source: *Eurobarometer* 1989.

Views on what the ideal roles of men and women in the family are. The results are given as a percentage.

	Both have an absorbing job and share roles equally	The wife has a less demanding job and does more of the housework	Husband has the job and the wife stays at home
Belgium	34	30	25
Denmark	53	26	12
Germany	26	34	32
Greece	43	28	23
France	45	29	24
Ireland	34	20	39
Italy	42	31	25
Luxembourg	20	30	39
Netherlands	43	28	23
Portugal	43	24	25
Spain	47	19	28
UK	48	31	18

Source: *Eurobarometer 1987.*

FRANCE

Background

France is Europe's largest country after the USSR. It borders on six countries and has coastlines on the Mediterranean, Atlantic and the Channel. With 55 million inhabitants the population density is one of the lowest in Europe. The geography, climate, history and culture are extremely varied, embracing regions as different as Brittany, Alsace, Provence and the Basque country.

There is a strong attachment to one's home region and a reluctance for people to transfer between regions, the exception being a move to Paris. Even if they have worked all their lives in Paris they will often consider themselves Parisian only if they were born there. True Parisians regard a transfer to the provinces as exile. It is also difficult to relocate French employees overseas and they find it harder to settle down than those from many other countries.

The North was originally populated by people of Germanic origin, with a system of customary law and speaking *langue d'oïl*. The South was populated by Mediterraneans, with a codified Roman law system and speaking a different language, *langue d'oc*. (*Oïl* and *oc* mean 'yes'. *Langue d'oïl* is the precursor of modern French — *Oïl* became *oui*). The boundary between the two civilisations runs very roughly from Bordeaux to Macon.

The North–South divide is complicated by differences between East and West. Western France from Brittany to Aquitaine has a strong Atlantic tradition that it shares with Britain and

Scandinavia. Geographically, it is characterised by ports and long, navigable rivers, economically by maritime trade. It was primarily the west that supplied the sailors, merchants and colonisers of North America. In contrast Eastern France belongs to continental Europe. It has strong historical and economic links with Germany, Switzerland and Italy. This is the industrial heartland of France, based on coal and mineral deposits and the Rhine.

Some observers have added yet another dimension to the diversity of France, this one based on a central core surrounded by an outer ring. With its many borders and seaports the outer ring has a mercantile, liberal, innovative and outward-looking culture susceptible to external influence and change. Meanwhile the inner core is rural, isolated, agricultural, protectionist and traditional.

These differences are said to illuminate contradictory strains in French mentality and behaviour. France is anything but a monolithic society, although it may appear so from Paris. It is a pluralist collection of economic, regional and political interest groups that coexist in a sometimes uneasy truce. Newcomers should not assume that everyone conforms to a Parisian stereotype.

Centralism

The political response to size and diversity is centralisation, derived not from the predominance of one powerful region suppressing the others — England, Prussia, Castile — but from the creation of an idea of statehood that transcends and absorbs regionalism and excludes any concept based on federalism or devolution. It is imbued from an early age in the education system that not only teaches but incorporates it into a national curriculum and examination system.

The chicken and egg question of whether centralism derives from a French mentality or vice versa can be endlessly debated. But it permeates French attitudes to all organisations including economic ones. Centralised, ordered, legalistic, elitist, the political structure is a model for business corporations. Vertical administration, clear-cut divisions, ordered hierarchies, central planning are features of companies as well as the state.

The basis of political centralism is a rigidly codified legal system, the *Code Napoléon*, established when rationalism was at its height. It is a monument to the belief that human reason can overcome the unpredictability of human behaviour. A battery of regulations make up an ordered framework of existence imposed from above. It is an intellectual, artificial, regulated set of rules drawn up to anticipate every possible contingency. If there is a gap between principle and reality it is filled, not with improvisation, but ever more refined orders and regulations.

However, the real world does not follow regulations. The antidote is '*Système D*'. ('D' stands for *débrouillard* — the art of overcoming obstacles, or beating the system.) French ingenuity in creating formal systems is matched by ingenuity in evading them. It is a principle which applies equally well to the business environment.

Attitudes to government

France has been a unified state with centralised political, educational and economic systems for 200 years, one of the more durable in Europe. To be French is to adhere to a much stronger and homogeneous set of values than countries in which a strong regionalism and a more recent national unity dilute a sense of national identity. There is a high degree of identification with the state. Concorde, the Channel Tunnel, are more than commercial projects but an embodiment of national pride.

The Government responds with political, economic and social nationalism. Protectionism of industry, reaching down to small scale industrial and agricultural enterprise, is a plank of economic policy. Direct and indirect intervention in industry is common. In many sectors the division between public and private sectors is blurred. Business expects government intervention in times of domestic crisis or to help ward off foreign incursion. This intervention, unlike say in the UK where it is reactive and forced by circumstance, is centrally planned and administered.

While individuals are generally preoccupied with outwitting the government, especially in matters of taxation, the attitude of business is based on respect. While government may not always deliver what business asks for at least there will be a well informed, reasoned answer that has the fundamental interest of business at heart. Civil servants are highly paid and enjoy social prestige. Government is sometimes regarded as politically motivated and manipulative but not dishonest. People coming from countries in which government is regarded as incompetent, obstructive or corrupt, will need to take this into account when working in France.

The links between government and business are personal as well as formal. Industry finds many of its leaders among the graduates of the Grandes Ecoles, which also supply the élite corps of civil servants. It is common to transfer back and forth between the two, the acquaintanceships thus formed being a vital ingredient of effectiveness in both spheres.

Foreign investment is closely controlled and monitored by the government. This has not prevented foreign multinationals gaining control of about a fifth of French industry, concentrating on modern technologies. They own about 80 per cent of the business machine industry, 70 per cent of oil and 60 per cent of agricultural machinery. While some of these companies behave like natives, others have introduced predominantly American management systems and style.

Labour market

Labour unions are highly politicised and adversarial. The most important are the pro communist CGT, the socialist CFDT and the right wing FO. But only about a fifth of the workforce is unionised, the lowest proportion in Europe and lower than the USA.

French labour laws, for the most part assembled in a Labour Code, the *Code du Travail*, are extensive and comprehensive. The work contract, *contrat du travail*, is strictly regulated as are the rules that protect the employee in case of dismissal. The attitude to these and other formalities is one of compliance as long as they do not stand in the way of what the management wishes to do.

If a company has more than 50 employees it is obliged by law to have a works committee *comité d'entreprise* chaired by the chief executive. Those with fewer than 50 employees often have one too. The number of employees elected to the committee ranges from three to fifteen in companies with over 10,000 employees. The role of the committee is not at the discretion of the chair but defined by law and the chief executive is personally liable if he or she neglects to hold the monthly meeting. The formalities of the comité d'entreprise are rigorously adhered to and enforced. The annual financial statement, and any other financial information required by law, must be submitted to the comité d'entreprise. There is a legal requirement for the company to respond to any questions raised by the committee and to provide regular information on the general state of the company. It has a consultative role on personnel matters such as pay, benefits, working conditions and terms of employment. It also operates staff social and welfare activities.

In small companies employee representatives on the committee (*Délégués du Personnel*) are elected by groups determined by skill, seniority or specialisation. In larger companies they are nominated by their union and play a political rather than a corporate role. Their ostensible task is to relay complaints about conditions of work in regular meetings with the employer and the comité d'entreprise and to brief employees with information.

While the rules are rigidly adhered to and there is considerable value in an orderly mechanism for communicating information and complaint, up and down, the same comments apply to how it works in practice as to other apparently legalistic elements in the corporate structure.

Organisation and structure

Limited liability companies can be either a stock company — *Société Anonyme* (S.A.) — or a private company — *Société à Responsabilité Limitée* (SARL). The management of the Société Anonyme can take two forms:

- A board of directors comprised of elected shareholders (*le Conseil d'Administration*) whose chairman (*le Président*) is chosen by the board and has complete managerial responsibility. The board may appoint one or several managing directors (*Directeur Général*) to assist the chairman.
- A dual management system consisting of a supervisory board (*Conseil de Surveillance*) and a management board of two to seven executives (*Directoire*). These executives are appointed by the supervisory board and manage the company under its control. The management board votes by majority.

The private company, SARL, is usually small with a maximum of 50 shareholders who appoint one or several managers (*le Gérant*).

French institutions of whatever size are highly centralised. Beneath a powerful Chief Executive, *le Président Directeur Général* (PDG), is a strict hierarchy of executives organised on functional lines with rigid chains of command. There are typically many more layers of middle management than in, say, a German or a Dutch company. All lines of communication and authority run vertically to the boss. Staff functions are there to advise the boss and not the line managers. Matrix management has had its day in most business cultures but in France it hardly saw the dawn. Interdepartmental liaison is cumbersome and wherever possible flows through the centre.

This means that when things go well they go very well indeed. The problem comes when things do not go well and response to changing situations is needed. Traditional French authority structures are unresponsive to varying conditions.

18

Problems tend to be pushed further up the line. Change in French organisations, as in French society, tends to be spasmodic and radical.

If corporate life were generally as formal as it appears on the surface it would be far more rigid and stifling than it is in practice. Rules and procedures are rarely broken but they are constantly distorted, manipulated and ignored if they do not serve the purpose for which they are intended. The plea for the special case — *le cas particulier* — is invariably acceded to. Beneath the apparent structure of the organisation there is usually an invigorating sub-culture based on informal networking and characterised by flexibility, scepticism and energy.

Le plan

Among capitalist countries France is the leading exponent of economic planning and does it better than any of the so-called centrally planned economies further east. Corporate strategic planning among companies is also far-reaching and detailed. The larger the company the more elaborate it is and the longer the time horizon. Nuclear power, high speed trains, the electronic industry are typical of long-term strategic investments carried out over many years according to a rigorous plan unaffected by changes in Government, the economy and, some would say, external circumstances. This is one reason why French industrial policy sometimes seems out of phase with that of other countries.

Planning tends to be inductive. It is a question of an intuitive vision for the future rather than a prediction. The PDG decides on the direction he wants to go and hands the detail over to specialists who draw up the plan. A deductive process, where ideas and data are gathered by line managers who participate in planning would be alien to the authority structure. The result is usually that managers do not own the plan and have no commitment to its implementation. Newcomers should find out what the plan is but not be surprised if their colleagues are getting on without it.

Le patron

The PDG is expected to be a strong authority figure with a high degree of technical competence. In a recent survey of European managers one of the questions was: 'Is it important for a manager to have at his fingertips precise answers to most of the questions that subordinates raise about their work?' Of Frenchmen, 60 per cent said it was, the highest percentage along with Italians. A French PDG shows much more attention to detail than equivalents in other countries. The boss naturally behaves in a way which in other countries would be considered dictatorial. It is difficult for bosses to admit that they are ignorant about something. Even in private diplomacy is needed to change his mind. Likewise the boss will rarely open his mind, much less his heart, to his subordinates or share his problems with them. At the same time subordinates will feel free to criticise and argue to a greater extent than in many other countries.

In dealing with subordinates it is better to err on the side of the directive as long as one's position is well-founded and logical. This is sometimes misinterpreted by outsiders as a need for autocratic leadership. Along with logic in the French mentality goes a deep and healthy scepticism. They are happy to be led but only in the right direction and for the right reasons. Respect for authority is based first and foremost on respect for competence. Strength of personality is rarely enough on its own.

Delegation

Job descriptions are usually a detailed list of tasks and reporting lines. Supervisors are expected to follow-up and chase progress. In keeping with the nature of hierarchy more emphasis is placed on supervision than.control systems.

The practice of regular performance appraisal is being introduced but progress is slow. They are usually trait based — punctuality, reliability and so on — rather than performance based. In an environment where performance is inextricably linked with the personal qualities of those doing the performing, appraisal implies personal criticism. Performance standards and targets are avoided as much as possible because they are potential weapons. Appraisal based on objective and collaborative target setting and feedback would require a considerable change in conventional working relationships.

A high degree of analysis, control and technical knowledge of the operations is required of line managers. They are expected to provide precise answers to questions, not approximations.

Teams

The concept of a team is a collection of specialists chosen for their competence in a given field under the command of an unequivocal leader. Professional relationships between colleagues are founded more on rivalry than collaboration. This begins in the highly competitive school environment which is based on getting over a series of ever higher hurdles. Learning to collaborate to solve problems is not an educational goal.

In business, competitiveness is fostered by strong vertical hierarchies. Far from refreshing, people find it disconcerting when others do not compete. They will not wait for a group consensus before taking an initiative. To those from more participative cultures this can appear deliberately provocative. Foreigners used to a team approach will usually have to adjust their expectations of working relationships.

Meetings

Meetings called by the manager will follow an established format with a detailed agenda. Their purpose is for briefing and coordination rather than a forum for debate or decision making. People will come well prepared for the contribution they are expected to make and be ready to fend off objections if they arise. Usually they will not expect to be seriously contradicted. In the public forum of a meeting, to question a proposal or an idea is to question the competence of the person who put it forward. Getting together at a meeting to kick ideas around, floating a few trial balloons, sorting a problem out together, is not common. There is too much personal risk and too great an opportunity to unleash the competitiveness which character-ises relationships between colleagues. The carefully drafted report objectivises ideas and reduces the chances of authors laying themselves open to attack.

If the input of others is needed it is most likely to be secured before the meeting takes place with the individuals concerned. Interaction between them is through the medium of the boss, whose contribution will probably have been made before the meeting and given prior approval. If the boss calls into question proposals in public it is taken as a sign of displeasure. A meeting, and any other 'public' occasion, is above all an opportunity for the boss to assert authority. Consensus is not a major objective. The primary purpose is clarification and assent.

Meetings may not be a spontaneous interchange but they are less time consuming than in team-oriented cultures and what they propose and discuss tends to be better thought out. Spontaneity and creativity take place on the lower level of communication in informal discussion between people who believe they can trust each other.

Meetings where there is not an established senior figure as chairman are less structured. Participants will feel free to leave the meeting, conduct side conversations and interrupt. There is little collegiate atmosphere. Contributions are assertive to the point of being combative and phrased to beat back opposition. If a decision is to be taken and some of the relevant people are missing it will be taken anyway and the others will be informed. However, the likelihood of their going along with it will be diminished.

Communication

As in most business cultures writing memos and letters and minutes is more often for self-defence than communication. In many companies dictating memos is regarded as a waste of time. People write their own or use the phone.

But studies and reports are a significant element in the decision making process. Oral presentations and discussions for disseminating information or gathering input for decisions is an Anglo-Saxon innovation. Circulation of reports for individual study and comment is more important. For this reason a high value is placed on their being comprehensive, clear, well-structured, well-written and well-presented.

This is not to say that communication is invariably stiff and formal. It happens on two levels. On the surface business relationships are conducted in what is considered to be a proper, orderly and professional way, uncluttered by personal relationships. This is what is meant by *sérieux*. But beneath this there is a complicated network of personal relationships, alliances and factions through which things actually get done. Off the record, informal contacts are very important. The skill of bosses in engineering them with their subordinates, despite the hierarchical barriers in their way, makes a major contribution to their effectiveness.

Upward mobility

At the summit of the educational system are the meritocratic Grandes Ecoles which provide the civil service and industry with its élite. They are practical and scientific and competition to get into them is very high. They provide not only an education but entry into a powerful and pervasive alumni network.

Considerable importance is attached to professional qualifications not only at the recruiting stage. The most prized discipline is mathematics in which French schools and universities excel. One senior French manager said that he would dearly like to employ more British mathematicians because they worked so well in teams but they did not have the technical ability to hold their own. Whatever this says about the relative worth of British and French mathematics, it is certainly illuminating about his priorities.

There is a bias towards purely academic qualifications as opposed to apprenticeships or on the job training. Technical qualifications, for example engineering, carry the highest status, followed by law and finance. Sales and marketing used not to attract the intellectually gifted but an increasing number of Grandes Ecoles like HEC and ESSEC are producing high calibre marketing graduates. Accountants have a lower status than in Anglo-Saxon countries and the finance director might not be a board member.

In-house training is underdeveloped compared with many countries and is concerned more with technical development than general management. However the government has recently intervened with a requirement that four per cent of the payroll has to be put into a training fund.

Job-hopping for experience or promotion is still unconventional. The predominant ethic is to remain with one company. This is reciprocated by a mixture of paternalism and the legal and administrative hurdles in the way of dismissing someone for anything other than gross misconduct.

There is a high degree of company loyalty. The company is a social unit in which each member has a well defined part. While French people like to feel individualistic and self-reliant they also need to feel part of a caring social unit. Family centred in private life they are company centred in business life. The cliché, beloved of chief executives, that their staff are a family is more applicable in France than Anglo-Saxon companies. Given the high proportion of family businesses it may well be factually true too.

Promotion is usually on the basis of seniority tempered with educational qualifications and competence. In organisations based on vertical hierarchy and specialisation it is rare to be promoted to different departments unless you are obviously being groomed for the top. In a large company it is difficult to work your way to the top from the back office or the factory floor. These positions are usually reserved for family members or graduates from the Grandes Ecoles. It has been estimated that three quarters of the senior managers of the 200 largest companies are the sons of wealthy families compared to one quarter in Germany and a tenth in the USA.

For outsiders the first requirement for acceptance is professionalism. New ideas and techniques are welcomed as long as they are well researched and logically argued and have a conceptual rigour. Their implementation depends primarily on personal relationships. Respect for the messenger is as important as for the message. It is unwise for outsiders to join in the internal politics of the organisation, but they should make every effort to get to know their colleagues well, and be known by them, before instituting change or asserting authority.

Attitudes and behaviour

'Intellectual' is not a term of abuse as it is in some other countries. French people enjoy abstract thought, theory, formulas and a degree of logic and analysis which often seems impractical to pragmatic thinkers like the British or the Dutch. Eclecticism is not an important element of mental discipline and there is a mistrust of pure pragmatism. One embarks from a central axiom and moves logically to a conclusion. They have been accused of preferring clarity to truth, words to facts and rhetoric to knowledge. They can be very stubborn and inflexible when confronted with the necessity for change unless they see an overall logic to it. They will tolerate impracticability more easily than inconsistency, an approach more suited to radical restructuring than gradual reform.

Despite a reputation for chauvinism the French are not hidebound by traditional ways of doing things. They are open to borrowing manners and style from anywhere as long as it is useful and, above all, elegant. They embrace novelty with enthusiasm, whatever its source. A French home and a French office are full of gadgets. Interactive video telephones, high speed trains, adventurous architecture like the Beaubourg or the Louvre pyramid cause excitement not scandal. Even the kitchen, for many the focus of French civilisation, has been invaded with microwaves and freezers, nouvelle cuisine and fast food.

Women

French women are increasingly represented in the management of retail and service industries and in areas such as law, finance and personnel. There remains considerable bias against them in industry and outside Paris.

Etiquette

Etiquette among colleagues varies according to generation, sex, the business the company is in, whether they are talking to Anglo-Saxons or have adopted an American style. Colleagues on about the same level tend to use first names in private but go back to second names in public or in front of the boss or at formal meetings. In more traditional companies second names are the rule all the time and for everyone. Among younger people the old formality is rapidly changing. Dress codes are variable, reflecting status or the type of business or whether it is Paris or the provinces. Often the most formal wear is reserved for visits to head office while out on the road or in a branch office style is more relaxed. Everybody shakes hands on meeting and parting, however well they know each other.

Language

A love of elegance applies above all to language. National pride increases sensitivity to incorrect use of the language, but they also find it genuinely jarring to hear it being massacred. While this is a reason to learn to speak it well it is not an excuse for not trying. It is more of a compliment to make an effort than an offence to speak it badly.

It may also be a necessity to speak French, however poorly. The French are almost as notoriously bad at languages as the British and Italians and for the same reason — they are badly taught in school. As far as English is concerned this is changing rapidly. There has been a noticeable change of attitude in recent years. Soon French children will begin to learn English at the age of seven and the syllabus is being made more practical.

They are less tolerant when French is written badly — and there is less excuse for making mistakes. It is worthwhile persuading typists to overcome their inhibitions about contra-dicting *le patron* and make corrections. Even slight memos and notes are written in a mandarin style that in other countries is the preserve of senior civil servants. You will rarely find colloquially written memos and reports in the recorded speech style favoured by Anglo-Saxons. This is partly a concern for professionalism and partly an emphasis on correct grammar and usage in school. To write correctly is a sign of education and breeding.

Punctuality

Punctuality depends on the social circumstances and the importance of the person to be kept waiting. About 15 minutes is the average slippage. They will change their timetables at short notice if subsequent engagements are more important.

Humour

French people prefer wit to the belly-laugh. They tend not to sit around swapping jokes. Their humour is more likely to be intelligent and satirical and at someone else's expense. The political jokes that are the forte of Latin and Slav humour are more common in the South.

At work, humour is rarely used on formal occasions or meetings. It is not usual for the PDG to warm up an audience with a couple of stories or sprinkle a presentation with jokes. If he does, they must be intelligent and dignified. Similarly at meetings, even relatively informal ones, humour is rarely used to make a point or release tension. It would be regarded as flippant. It is not that business or money are too serious to be made fun of. They are treated with a healthy disrespect, not to say cynicism, outside the office. But to do so at a business meeting is not *sérieux*. The personal remarks that pepper Anglo-Saxon conversations with colleagues, however friendly or amusing, are regarded as aggressive and rude and should be avoided.

Socialising

Lunch with a superior is rare and formal. Bosses do not socialise with their subordinates at work or after hours. Getting together over sandwiches in the boardroom or going out for a beer or a game of golf would be very unusual. Senior managers socialise with those of equivalent status in other companies.

The traditional two-hour lunch break to give people time to go home to eat with their families is under threat from the commuter style of living imposed by bigger cities, industrial developments and office parks. Even if you cannot get home, lunch is still regarded as 'private time' and food as deserving the main attention. While a sandwich on the desk or a quick hamburger round the corner is becoming more common, lunch is usually for relaxing at length on one's own or with friends.

The working lunch and even the fashionable working breakfast are becoming more widespread but they are innovations and more of an intrusion on personal life than, say, in Anglo-Saxon countries. This applies also to home entertaining. Foreigners who are used to sharing meals with colleagues should not feel slighted if it does not often happen. The exception is in companies large enough to have staff restaurants, the more innovative being single status. They will be used by everybody except the most senior managers.

More paternalistic companies will also organise social events for the staff through the works committee. Christmas parties and presents for children, summer camp, excursions abroad for workers, are usually paid for or subsidised by the company. More senior managers may make a token appearance but among themselves will keep personal lives separate from business relationships.

Office parties are rare and usually confined to celebrating transfer and promotion. Company loyalty is valued highly so leaving parties are not normal and paid for by the leaver, off the premises.

Personal relationships are regarded as important for their own sake. French people believe that there is more to life than the job. Hard work is admired but workaholism is not. While the affectation of regularly working late is creeping into Parisian working habits, there is a clear division between private and business lives. Weekends and vacation days, sport, cultural activities and family life are very important. Colleagues are

expected to be lively and interesting companions, well informed and appreciative of the good things of life as well as
successful at their jobs.

GERMANY

Regionalism

The *Länder* which make up the Federal Republic, and the associated *Land* of West Berlin, have real political and economic independence. There are noticeable differences in lifestyle and temperament between them but it is difficult to identify a simple geographical pattern. There is a north-south divide, with northerners following the custom of dismissing southerners as lazy and soft while the southerners reciprocate with taunts of dour and dull. There is a less tangible East-West contrast between the solid Saxons and cosmopolitan Rhine-landers.

Germany is better thought of as a patchwork, with enclaves and cities reflecting the tribalism and eccentricities of the old dukedoms and principalities. There are influences of a more recent vintage too. Systems of local government vary, depending on whether municipalities fell under the British, French or American sector after the war. In the same period an influx of 14 million refugees from Russian occupation added to the cocktail. By the time this book is in print, the map is likely to have been radically altered again.

Germany has several capitals, depending on your interest. Berlin is the official capital while Bonn is the centre of government. Frankfurt is for banking and finance, Hamburg for trade, Munich for sunrise industries, society and the arts, Düsseldorf-Dortmund-Essen for heavy industry. If you want to know about the largest automobile industry in Europe you have to go to Munich (BWM), Stuttgart (Daimler Benz, Porsche,

Mercedes), Wolfsburg (VW) and Cologne (Ford, GM). If you are interested in publishing you have to go to Munich, Frankfurt, Stuttgart, Hamburg and, for the biggest publishing group in Europe, the small town of Gütersloh, the headquarters of Bertelsmann. There is no dominating metropolis. This is why communications are so good and why road and rail networks are in a convenient matrix rather than a centralised spider's web. And why Germany has more and bigger trade fairs than other countries.

National identity

In the past hundred years Germans have gone through the menu of political systems including monarchy, empire, republic, dictatorship, federal democracy and democratic republic. If there is any consistency, it is the determination to exploit whatever is on hand to the limit of its potential. In the British Social Attitudes Special International Report, (1989), British and Germans were asked to rank various reasons for which they could be proud of their respective nationalities. In similar proportions the British gave the Monarchy as their first choice, with 37 per cent, and the Germans the *Grundgesetz* or 'basic law' with 30 per cent.

Second place in Germany, with 17 per cent, went to economic achievement while in Britain it ranked bottom with 2 per cent. Germans take business very seriously indeed, which those coming from countries with less regard for it would do well to bear in mind. They are justifiably proud of German abilities and achievements — some self-critical German commentators have said too proud, if not to the point of arrogance, then certainly to the point of complacency. A newcomer will soon come across the firm conviction that German products, German management, the German way of doing things is best.

Government intervention

Whatever the reasons for German economic success, a market economy free of Government intervention is not one of them. Apart from state monopolies in most public services the

Federal Government has major shareholdings in hundreds of German companies. In addition the Länder have proactive and interventionist policies often amounting to direct shareholdings. Regional and industrial subsidies are extensive and financed by one of the highest rates of corporate taxes in Europe.

The attitude to government participation in industry is not based on ideology but on a sense of partnership with the business community. It is this sense of community of interest which has undermined the privatisation attempts of the current government. It extends to the local level where local authorities, unions, schools, banks and businesses combine on a town, district and *Land* level to establish policies of mutual benefit.

Government intervention in business is most noticeable to the outsider in the panoply of regulations. It may not be the most regulated business environment in Europe but it is certainly the one in which regulations are most adhered to. In addition to regulations there are a host of guidelines and principles covering every aspect of running a business. In the unlikely event that a loophole is discovered it is customary not to exploit it but to refer to the appropriate authority for a ruling.

Some sections of the business community look enviously at other countries' moves towards deregulation and the increased competition that ensues. The counter-argument is that a genuinely competitive market can only exist if it is regulated. The Law Against Restraints on Competition is particularly strong and energetically enforced by the Federal Cartel Office. Its principal brief is to guard against the abuse of market dominance which it does by preventing companies from achieving a dominant position in the first place. Mergers and acquisitions of whatever size come under close scrutiny and the onus is on the companies to disprove the immediate assumption that their association will be detrimental to the marketplace. Unless the particular market is highly fragmented, horizontal mergers are unlikely to succeed.

The banks

Banks dominate business. At the top is the Bundesbank whose influence over the financial markets combines dirigism with meticulous information gathering, regulation and day-to-day control. Its authority is underpinned by obvious competence and independence from government, not forgetting the strength of the Deutschmark.

The big three, Deutsche, Dresdner and Commerzbank, combine the roles played in other countries by commercial bank, investment bank, merchant bank, savings bank, stockbroker and institutional investor. They are aptly described as 'universal banks'. Their strength derives from the immediate post-war years when the shortage of investment capital meant that bank finance was the only source of equity as well as working capital. In addition to the big three there are other banks no less influential on a *Land* level.

The banks' role of principal provider of funds, while it may serve well at times of economic crisis, exacerbates the difficulty in good times of finding capital for new ventures. Their natural conservatism and the lack of an active and independent stockmarket tends to stifle entrepreneurial growth and innovation.

The benefits of collaboration between government, banks and business are seen to outweigh the dangers of a conflict of interest. Businessmen from countries where banks and government are kept at arm's length or played off against each other need to modify their customary attitudes. A closely woven network of connections and loyalties and an innate distaste for stepping out of line means that those who break ranks quickly find themselves isolated.

Family companies

Anti-trust laws, the tight grip of banks over the stock market and strong regionalism have preserved the position of the family-owned small and middle sized company. Foreigners working with these companies may find more of a paternalistic environment than they are used to at home. They may find a sense of social responsibility and concern for long-term employee welfare that is alien to their experience. They may also feel excluded from policy making among family interests outside the forum of professional management. A constant challenge for German companies is to bridge the gap between the family firm and multi-disciplined professional management.

Long-termism

The dominating position of government, banks and closely held family companies means that Germany provides few pickings for stock market operators. Hostile takeover bids are almost unknown and it is extremely difficult to enter the German market by acquisition. While this will be deplored by those who believe that predators maintain the health of the herd, and the financial health of shareholders, it does mean that managers can devote their time and energy to managing the business instead of fighting off bids, planning management buyouts or worrying if they will have a job next year. They can afford to take a longer-term view than those preoccupied with tomorrow's share price and the quarterly results. They will take a strategic view of the development of their market without the pressure for immediate returns. They have to concentrate on achieving long-term growth internally rather than through acquisition or manipulation of assets. This is one reason, coupled with high labour costs, why continuous capital investment is an article of faith.

Industrial relations

While unions are no more welcomed by management than in other countries, they are acknowledged as an inevitable and necessary member of a partnership. While both sides are imbued with a sense of social responsibility and the admission that what is good for one side is similarly good for the other, they are also circumscribed by a comprehensive legal framework.

About 40 per cent of the workforce is unionised, with a preponderance towards heavy industry, steel and mining. Most belong to one of 17 unions in the Trade Union Federation (DGB) which are organised according to industry, not craft.

Full scale strikes during negotiations are rare and a last resort following prescribed and detailed arbitration and ballotting procedures. More frequent, although still uncommon, are short work stoppages during negotiations with individual companies. They rarely last for more than a few hours and are designed to underline a point rather than disrupt production. A favourite period for a work stoppage is 48 hours beginning four o'clock on a Friday afternoon.

Restrictions on union activity are balanced by stringent employee protection and welfare laws. Dismissal and layoffs are complicated and expensive to carry out. But the area which management finds most tiresome is the system of worker participation, *Mitbestimmung*. This provides for elected employee representation on the *Aufsichtsrat*, or supervisory board of outside directors.

Any company employing more than five people must set up a *Betriebsrat* or works council if the employees request it. It is composed solely of employees elected by secret ballot. It must be consulted by management every three months on all changes affecting working conditions including production methods and new investment, as well as personnel questions such as working hours, holiday schedules, incentive payments and so on. It must also be consulted about hiring, firing and transferring employees. By law, management again has the last word but in practice is best advised to maintain a constructive relationship. There is a saying that managers get the Betriebsrat chairman they deserve. Sooner or later in their careers managers will be judged on their ability to work with the Betriebsrat while keeping it in line.

Business organisation and structure

Business organisations are oligarchical. Power is concentrated in a small number of people at the top. Public corporations (AG) and limited companies (GmbH) with over 500 employees, have a supervisory board (*Aufsichtsrat*) which consists of up to 20 members. It appoints the management board (*Vorstand*) which has the last word on management policy matters. Since the directors (*Vorstandsmitglieder*) are re-appointed every four years they tend not to exercise this prerogative too freely. In smaller private companies which do not have to have an Aufsichtsrat the directors are appointed directly by the shareholders and are known as *Geschäftsführer*.

All decisions of any importance are taken by the Vorstandsmitglieder or Geschäftsführer. (They are not to be confused with *Direktoren* who are the top level of middle management.) While each of them may have a particular expertise or functional role they share responsibility jointly for the management of the company. Because the Vorstand is legally collective, the chairman (*Sprecher* or *Vorsitzende*) is less powerful than his equivalent in other countries.

The participative element of German organisational culture stops here. Below the Vorstand or Geschäftsführung there is a strict vertical hierarchy. The organisation and the individual's role within it are logical, methodical and compartmentalised. Functions and the relationship between them are thoroughly defined and documented. Procedures, routines, doing things by the book are important. Cutting corners, taking initiatives, skimping on the formalities are frowned upon. Newcomers are well advised to stick closely to the rules until they are absolutely sure of the acceptable way in which they can be tempered by pragmatism.

What would lead to a bureaucratic nightmare in other cultures works in Germany because of a respect for perfectionism extending to all areas of business and private life. However, when the unexpected does happen, even in the best run organisations they are less well equipped to handle it. They look for the mechanism that has already been worked out and if it does not exist they tend to be at a loss. It also means that German organisations are not good at maintaining a process of constant and regular change. They are better suited to a manufacturing environment where major decisions have a long life span.

Planning

Germans are uneasy with uncertainty and ambiguity and unquantifiable risk. Experience and temperament have fostered a strong fear of insecurity. Faced with the choice they will take the most conservative option. Opportunism is seen less as a talent than a failure to organise.

Planning is seen as the responsibility of senior management and not of those lower down in the organisation. If there are several people involved it requires constant discussion and complete consensus. Anyone with expertise and knowledge will be asked to give a considered opinion and will be seriously listened to. While studies and analysis are important these are tempered by intuition and common sense. It will be a cautious decision, loaded with fall-back positions, contingency plans and alternatives, and subject to empirical testing. The approach is best described as 'systematically pragmatic'.

Once the decision is collectively made it is translated into rigorous, comprehensive action steps which are carried out to the letter without questioning. Alternative solutions are not encouraged to permeate upwards or sideways from people not recognised as qualified to contribute to them.

Leadership

Germans look for strong, decisive leadership from somebody who knows what he is talking about. There is a universal deference to people in authority and subordinates will rarely contradict or criticise their boss. Superiors expect to be obeyed and in return are expected to provide unequivocal direction. It would be wrong to regard this as subservience. Orders are obeyed out of respect for the boss's functional role and his competence.

Some may take advantage of this to indulge a dictatorial manner. Although it is certainly not done to answer back, such behaviour is no more acceptable to. Germans than it is to others. Greater store is set by managers who rely on technical competence rather than force of personality. People from countries where outbursts of temper are a privilege of seniority and a sign of getting tough should know that in Germany they are regarded as uncouth and a sign of weakness.

Doing the minimum to get by is abhorred at all levels of the organisation, especially senior management. It is important that the boss be seen to be working hard, getting his hands dirty. While the upwardly mobile expect to be rewarded, the chance to take it easy while others get on with it is not associated with promotion.

Employees readily obey instructions but they prefer to be left to carry them out without interference. Delegation is clear, precise and preferably written.

Relationships between bosses and subordinates tend to be distant and awkward. While bosses may deliberately keep an open door most people are too intimidated to walk through it. Younger employees often want their bosses to be more accessible. They expect more participation and feedback and have fewer inhibitions about asking for it, which older style bosses have difficulty in coping with.

The kind of appraisal system in which performance and progress are frankly discussed is not common in traditional companies. Employees do not expect to share in the setting of objectives. They are censorious about even minor failings, especially if a procedure has been broken or ignored. Feedback has to be precise and objective since criticism is neither given nor received easily.

Teams

The concept of a team is a group of individuals each with a given expertise under a strong leader with a specific objective and a recognised place in the overall organisation. Ad hoc groups across hierarchical lines do not obtain whole-hearted commitment. They have to be properly constituted, have a place in the timetable and the organisation chart and not add to the members' workload. Those used to more fluid ways of working should not misinterpret reluctance to cooperate as of lack of goodwill and certainly not idleness. It derives from a strong sense that everything should be part of a methodical pattern.

Meetings

Germans are much more relaxed in individual discussions than at large meetings. Unless it is a dire emergency, meetings of any sort will be scheduled weeks in advance. They are formal with agenda and minutes. There is possibly a polite period of small talk first while a secretary serves tea or coffee but thereafter they are strictly functional.

Meetings between boss and subordinates are usually for coordination or briefing or formal ratification of decisions. The decision making process — identification of the problem, consideration of alternative solutions and so on — will have been largely carried out beforehand by the relevant experts. The meeting will be dominated by the senior person. It is less likely to be a forum for upward communication or alternative opinion than a mechanism for giving orders. Divergent opinions are rarely welcome — differences should have been resolved in advance or saved until later.

Compliance rather than consensus is expected. It is assumed that everyone will work to implement decisions regardless of how they feel about them. When giving instructions it is not important to explain and persuade but it is very important to be clear and decisive.

Meetings between peers or at a senior level, when a major decision or policy issues are being discussed, tend to have a different character. There is much more, even debate. Nevertheless, it is important to come very well prepared and not to comment on things you are not qualified to speak about. Proffering uninformed opinions, dogmatic statements and premature conclusions, however inspired or elegant, is to be avoided. It is unwise to spring something new on a formal meeting. It is more acceptable to remain silent if you have nothing to say than make a contribution for the sake of it.

Communication

Communication is primarily top-down and on a need-to-know basis. Information is required to flow upwards only when asked for. Due to a pervading deference to authority, people accept that superiors should be better informed than they are. While there is a hunger for information and there is no shortage of politicking, they do not suspect great secrets and conspiracies. The main concern is to get on with the job.

Many German companies thrive on a massive amount of written communication, elaborating and confirming what has been discussed and agreed face-to-face. Such communication always used to be dictated and typed but with the escalating cost it is increasingly acceptable to use handwritten internal communication until electronic internal mail systems become more widespread.

Germans have not mastered a telephone manner, unlike Latin neighbours who can be as loquacious and intimate over the phone as around the table. Germans are more inhibited, and especially on conference calls. They miss the cues and feedback and the setting.

Upward mobility

There is no dominant élite, no equivalent of the Grandes Ecoles and prestigious universities. In an organisational culture which values professional competence it is not uncommon for people to rise through the ranks from humble beginnings to the Vorstand. Those with a technical background have the best chance to do so.

An engineer has a higher status than a marketing or financial specialist. Higher education, both in the highly developed apprenticeship system and at the universities, is mainly vocational. Seventy per cent of the workforce is occupationally qualified. Training, predominantly technological, continues throughout an employee's career. Management education as a separate discipline is not viewed with great enthusiasm. Companies prefer to instil their own methods.

In most companies a fast track career is rare. There is a

permanence of position and a recognisable prospect of planned, steady progression. Getting ahead is not just a question of what you know. The British Social Attitudes Special International Report (1989) stated that when asked to rank the factors influencing getting ahead in life Germans put education first, ambition second, knowing the right people third, hard work a surprising fourth and ability fifth. This is a glimpse of a not wholly technocratic society but one where competitiveness and who you know are important.

Job hopping is more common between foreign owned companies than among family owned companies or the large conglomerates. There is a greater concern for job security than promotion. Most prefer to stay in their home town or region which limits the scope for moving. In some industries it is seen as a major professional weakness and even job rotation is viewed with scepticism. A move is usually more to obtain further technical experience or qualification rather than to leap up the ladder of seniority.

The rewards of success are not noticeably financial. The spread of earnings between the highest and the lowest paid is the smallest in the EC. Performance related pay, at any level, is not a significant feature of salary structures. People are expected to do the best job they can and be rewarded by eventual promotion.

Attitudes and behaviour

Germans are competitive and ambitious. They do not identify or sympathise with failure. It is shameful to be out of work and bankruptcy is a social and professional stigma. They place a great deal of importance on individual success and its outward trappings. The car you drive, the size of the office, where you take holidays are important.

There is a clear demarcation between private and business life. They leave work as punctually as they arrive and rarely take work home. They do not like being called at home on business unless there is a very good reason. People at all levels take their full holiday entitlement and they do not keep in touch with the office when they are away or expect to be called.

There is not the same alliance-building across boundaries as in many companies. Informal contacts are more within functions rather than across boundaries. But they are frequent and important. On a personal basis colleagues like to know a lot about each other. They are very liberal and uncensorious about private life but they like to know who they are dealing with.

The highly organised career structure of German companies limits the potential for individual advancement. It is not likely that a colleague or a subordinate will suddenly be whisked ahead of you or that an outsider will be brought in. This reduces the threat of competition and cultivates an attitude of cooperation based on mutual self-interest. People will associate with and help those who are capable and likely to succeed. There is a high value placed on *Kollegialität* coupled with a strong distaste for non-conformism. At the outset newcomers will be treated with a certain degree of mistrust until they establish their credentials, their ability and whether they pose a threat. Once they are established they will be treated a lot less defensively than in less structured organisations.

Women

The people who are least likely to make it to the top are women. Another survey, Eurobarometer of 1988, reported that among Europeans, Germans were found to hold the most traditional views of the role of women in society. While the old admonition that they should stick to *Kinder, Küche und Kirche* has been fast fading, it has not been replaced by a greater acceptance of women in positions of responsibility in business. There are some structural reasons why they may find it harder: the bias against girls taking technical subjects at school; the time it takes to get a university degree; the lack of sex discrimination laws are some. But the fundamental reason is that German males are chauvinist.

Etiquette

Some newcomers find the stiffness and formality of social and business contact inhibiting. Germans have a strong sense of privacy and their protective shell extends much further into public life than in many other countries.

There is a strong sense of community and social conscience which to some may appear based more on social tidiness than genuine neighbourliness. There is a great antipathy towards stepping out of line, out of one's prescribed role. Eccentricity of the mildest sort will attract open criticism. While there is an instinctive dislike of personal confrontation there is no hesitation in pointing out to someone that he or she does not meet acceptable standards of behaviour. This may be for something as trivial — in your eyes — as taking off a jacket at a meeting or parking in the wrong place. Policing each other's behaviour is not seen as offensive but a social duty.

Unlike some countries where the jacket is worn as a sign to fellow commuters that you have a job, and then left hanging on the back of the door until it is time to go home, in most German offices you keep it on and buttoned up unless you are alone. Shirt sleeves are a sign of relaxation, not getting down to work.

Public behaviour is in sharp contrast with the informality and warmth of private life and genuine friendships. Intimacy is not freely given but is much more durable than the instant variety peddled by more informal societies. There is a strong desire for belonging, for *Bruderschaft*. Sometimes this spills over into sentimentality but for the most part is kept on a tight rein.

This demarcation between public and private is illustrated by the way people interact. The general rule is for everyone to address each other by *Herr* or *Frau* followed either by their last name or, if they have one, their title and then the last name. Frau is almost always used instead of Fräulein for single women. The title is either a professional qualification or a position in the company. It is a lapse of etiquette not to use a person's title, if they have one, or to get it wrong. If in doubt, look on their business card.

If you are speaking German, the polite plural, the *Sie* form, is almost always used. Close colleagues of a younger generation tend to use first names among themselves. At a meeting, in front of strangers, or in front of the boss, they will revert to second names or titles. The informal singular *Du* is only used by agreement among close friends and the transition is a significant event. It marks the entry into each other's jealously guarded 'private space' and should never be taken lightly. It is a sign that familiarity at work has expanded into a lasting personal friendship. It is usually initiated by the senior person, in rank or age, and is marked by a ritual — a drink or a meal and a formal agreement. It is usually the result of something shared — a project, a business trip, a specific piece of collaboration. The friendship is expected to continue even if careers take you different ways.

If you are American or British do not be surprised that your German colleagues have read their etiquette guides too — probably more thoroughly than you have. They will be prepared to adopt an easy Anglo-Saxon familiarity but only while they are speaking English. If you switch to German you should revert to the formal style. If you are both using English as a second language then you should probably remain formal.

A notable exception is among computer specialists. There is something about working with computers, perhaps because it is a young profession, that induces informality in dress and manners the world over.

However informal the relationship, politeness and good manners are essential. Colleagues expect each other to be reserved but friendly. They are careful to greet each other properly in the morning and evening and also at mid-day with *Mahlzeit*, when they go to lunch.

Punctuality

It is very important to be punctual, which means on the dot. Only in academic circles is the professor's ten minutes delay acceptable. It is also acceptable to leave work on time. There is a strong sense that the relationship between the company and the employee is contractual. You are paid for so many hours and you work as hard as you can, but that is the end of it. There is no particular kudos for working over unless you are paid for it or there is a deadline to meet.

Humour

The old canard about humourless Germans is not borne out by acquaintance, whether of wry Hamburgers or witty Rheinlanders or jocular Bavarians. But levity does not belong at the workplace. Like so many aspects of German life, humour is strictly compartmentalised. The more formal the occasion, the less humour is acceptable.

Far from putting Germans at their ease, joking among strangers or new acquaintances often makes them feel uncomfortable. At meetings or presentations, while an American or a Briton might feel obliged to sprinkle speeches or presentations with jokes, or an Italian or a Frenchman would indulge in occasional witticisms, a German remains consistently serious.

In some countries people feel they can relax more as they get more senior. In Germany the opposite happens. Seniority is a mantle of responsibility which the holder must be seen to deserve and take seriously.

Among close colleagues in private there is banter and joking. It is usually sharp and biting and directed towards incompetence, mistakes and non-conformity. It is rarely facetious, especially about money or business, and never self-deprecating. To admit inadequacy even in jest is incomprehensible.

Socialising

When colleagues get together after hours great store is set by *Gemütlichkeit*, a combination of camaraderie and having a good time. The ease with which it is indulged varies between less inhibited southerners and the more low-key northerners.

At the workplace colleagues will often lunch together, especially if there is a staff canteen. This is not usually an opportunity for networking or talking shop. Although staff restaurants are often single status people will tend to keep the same company at the same table every day. A drink after work is common but not a regular end to the working day and rarely across rank. Many large companies have a '*Kasino*', or club, for senior managers.

Office parties are frequent but remain on a restrained, formal level. Birthdays are often celebrated with coffee and cakes or drinks in the office after hours. There is a constant chink of collection envelopes for birthday presents which are formally presented and must always be greeted with surprise. The annual Christmas party is not an opportunity to show the real you underneath the business suit. People are on their best behaviour. If someone were to get drunk or flirt outrageously it would not be forgotten. If things get lively at all it is at the very end of the evening when the bosses have left.

While Germans can be very hospitable towards business partners from abroad, and expect reciprocity, there is little mingling among colleagues out of hours and even less between ranks. Lunching with the boss usually takes place in the context of a business trip, a fair or a similar occasion when the stiffness of formal invitations and the danger of favouritism can be avoided.

If German working life seems dull and overregulated to people used to informality and confusion, there is circumstantial evidence that Germans share this opinion. They may work hard when they work but statistically they put in fewer hours than fellow Europeans. They are not fond of unpaid overtime, clockwatch at the end of the day, rush off home without lingering with colleagues. It is frequently difficult to contact colleagues on a Friday afternoon, especially in the south.

Carnival, or *Fastnacht* or *Fasching*, gives an interesting glimpse of another side of German character. It is associated mainly with Catholic areas and cities like Cologne and Mainz but is celebrated to some degree in most areas of Germany, including Frankfurt. The jollity is not confined to leisure hours. People come to the office in funny costumes, poke fun at their bosses, crack rude jokes. On women's day — the Thursday before Shrove Tuesday — men are advised to come to work with old ties as women will cut them off in symbolic revenge for the discrimination they suffer throughout the rest of the year. Colleagues eat and drink together and generally indulge in disorder and insubordination and Gemütlichkeit until it is over and they go back to sobriety and formality for the rest of the year.

ITALY

The unification of Italy began in 1870 when King Victor Emmanuel put an end to foreign domination for the first time since the Goths and vandals invaded the Roman Empire. Since then the reconciliation of rival cities, regions and interest groups has been painstaking. Many people still speak Italian in public and their own dialect at home. The Tuscan version of the original Latin predominates because it was the written language of Dante. If the economy is the German's principal source of national pride and the monarchy the Englishman's, cultural achievement is the Italian's.

While each village and town asserts its individuality some broad distinctions can be made. The officially recognised division is between the industrialised north and the under-developed south, the Mezzogiorno, which officially begins just to the south of Rome. Northerners say that it includes Rome. The two regions have markedly different attitudes to life and business. The stereotypical northerner is preoccupied with work and money, the southerner with power and the good life. To northerners the southerners suck their profits away in subsidies and handouts. To southerners the northerners are money-grubbers who exploit the workforce and suck their savings away for their factories.

Families

Italy is a matrix of interests and loyalties. Horizontally divided into regions it is vertically divided by factionalism. All aspects of Italian life are dominated by rival interest groups — political parties, public and private sector, employers and unions, church and state. Affiliation to at least one interest group is essential. Belonging to a political party or the church or a trade union or the Mafia or the Camorra or a masonic lodge or a trade association or a village is not a sociable association of like minds or like interests but an economic necessity. The most important affiliation is to family. Family ties remain more important than in any other European country with the possible exception of Spain and are the basis of the large number of self-employed and small businesses.

Affiliation, and the rights and obligations that go with it, replaces what passes for a wider social awareness in countries whose political and social institutions are more universally accepted. There are national policies in abundance but they do not percolate to the level of ordinary life.

Political framework

In most countries the exercise of power is rarely transparent but in Italy it is especially opaque. National government is in a state of permanent paralysis. On paper there is a well structured democratic system based on a comprehensive written constitution, an active presidency, and two elected houses. But the balance of power between them is so finely calculated that legislation can be batted between them for years. Add a multiplicity of parties, proportional representation, and a sophisticated lobbying and sponsorship system of economic and regional interest groups and the result is what is euphemistically described as a stable coalition and is in fact a permanent stand-off.

Really important issues, such as divorce, nuclear power, or pollution control, by-pass the whole logjam by means of national referenda. Another solution to central government inertia is decentralisation. There are 20 regions which have considerable autonomy in health, education and police. In addition elected local authorities in the numerous *comuni* have significant spending power, although Rome keeps control of funding.

Public figures are treated with respect and respond with an imposing dignity but this should not be misinterpreted. It is part of the game. Pomp and ceremony pander to a love of the dramatic, a source of entertainment. But they bear no relationship to the respect which authority figures command in practice. Government is popularly viewed as a group of separate cliques working for themselves. It is sometimes said that this attitude results from centuries of foreign rule through cumbersome bureaucracies. The payment of taxes is seen not as a duty to the community but as an exaction to be evaded. This is perhaps a rationalisation of something which goes deeper into Italian social values, namely a healthy mistrust of formal institutions of any sort, even ones in which they directly participate. At the same time there is a genuine enthusiasm for the EC. Brussels is a remedy for ungovernability, just as Vienna and Madrid had been. Only this time Italians can have their share of the power that goes with it.

The influence of political parties extends deep into economic and daily life. They exercise considerable power through their control of appointments to a wide range of jobs from cabinet minister to municipal employee to middle management of the many state owned companies. Patronage, or *raccomandazione*, along with the trading of favours and influence and votes and other inducements is a normal part of business life in the public sector. Private business has the same ambivalent relationship with the tentacular public sector as the individual towards government.

The political environment not only affects the conduct of business but also exemplifies attitudes which pervade the business environment. Virtually nothing of importance is done according to the book. As for corporate loyalty, the idea of working to make money for an impersonal organisation without extracting as much personal benefit as possible is not widely held.

State intervention

Despite this attitude and the experience of some of the most inefficient public services in Europe, Italians remain resolutely in favour of government intervention. Over 90 per cent are in favour of ownership or control of electricity, transport and banking and over 80 per cent of steel and the car industry. A majority consistently advocates government provision of jobs and legislation for wage and price control. Between the government and monopolistic private interests the government is considered the lesser of two evils.

The involvement of Government in the economy is already considerable. Government spending as a proportion of GDP is the highest in the EC. This is mainly in the form of social security and similar transfer payments. And yet, another paradox, Italians are much less directly dependent on the public sector for their livelihood. Only one in five employees are in public service occupations as opposed to just over one in three in the UK and just under one in three in the USA and Germany.

An even greater paradox, at least for those who believe that government has an influence on economic performance, is the success of the economy. Despite the inefficiencies and distortions and shortcomings of the public sector, Italy is claimed to have taken Britain's place as the fifth largest economy in the world, behind Germany and France.

But how do they know? Up to a third of economic activity is in the 'grey' or black market and by definition outside the scope of official statistical departments. Like so much that purports to pass for hard fact in Italy it is an estimate. No statistic, including those in this book, should be taken as more than an approximation.

Public and private sectors

The extensive state involvement in industry is primarily though the intermediary of three state holding companies — IRI, ENI and EFIM. The difference between nationalisation in Italy and other countries is that the real control is in the hands of the political parties and not the state bureaucracy. IRI, the largest of the three, is a Christian Democrat stronghold, ENI a socialist and EFIM up for grabs.

These companies are highly diversified conglomerates with interests ranging from lame duck industries such as steel and mining and shipbuilding to profitable companies in high tec engineering, food processing, banking, consumer goods, tourism and newspapers. Political expediency hampers the rationalisation of ailing industries in areas of high unemployment. It also discourages privatisation which would undermine the economic power base of the controlling parties.

The private sector is dominated by a small number of family owned companies of international standing such as Fiat, Olivetti and Benetton. Controlled by the *Condottieri* — industrialists like Agnelli, De Benedetti, Berlusconi, Giardini — they are more like family companies on a large scale than professionally managed, widely held corporations. They are diversified conglomerates. The Agnelli family for example has controlling interests not only in Fiat but in sectors as diverse as telecommunications, construction and publishing. Cross holdings between families discourage political intervention and foreign takeover.

The backbone of the economy is the thousands of small and medium sized private firms in the North. Their owners resist amalgamation partly for independence and partly for financial realism. It is more profitable to keep things in the family and to stay small enough to employ the officially self-employed, to avoid social security charges, to pay workers in cash, to use outworkers, to keep out of the hands of bankers and unions. Productivity in this sector is several times greater than in the state sector and strikes are a rarity.

For similar reasons large sectors of the economy remain artisanal and dispersed in small independent workshops. They exercise economic power and benefit from economies of scale by belonging to cooperatives, professionally managed and with substantial investment in plant and equipment. The retail trade, agriculture and construction industries are dominated by cooperatives, themselves grouped into consortia.

Industrial relations

All companies with more than 15 employees are obliged by law to have a works committee, the *consiglio de fabbrica*. It has the right to monitor conditions of work, investment plans and so on as well as being the channel for grievances.

About 40 per cent of the officially calculated workforce is unionised. Unions are highly politicised and membership is on political rather than craft or industry lines. The relationship between management and unions is confrontational. Both unions and employers are strongly averse to the idea of worker participation. In addition to the three largest unions — Christian Democrat, Communist and Social Democrat, there are a host of smaller unions and workers' committees which bedevil industrial relations, especially in the public sector. It is these smaller unions which are mainly responsible for the high rate of strikes. That the unions have failed in their essential mission is evidenced by the inequality of earnings. The differential between the highest and lowest paid is over a third greater than in Germany and the UK.

There are two labour markets. The offical one is highly regulated with a strong bias in favour of the employee in the areas of recruitment, redundancy and dismissal, although the jobs-for-life environment of the seventies has been seasoned with realism and declining union power. The unofficial labour market in which an estimated 25 per cent of the workforce is engaged, is by definition unregulated.

Financing

Risk capital is in short supply from institutional sources. New ventures are based on private funds and expand through retained profits. The Milan stock exchange is small, poorly regulated and dominated by a few family interests. Banks dominate the financing of industry under the control of the Banca d'Italia which has the distinction of being free from political interference and suspicion of corruption.

Banks are highly regulated. They are not allowed to participate in the ownership of commercial companies. Short-term banks which provide retail services and working capital finance are prevented from making medium-term loans. These are the preserve of the medium- and long-term credit institutions.

Even so, there is no unified banking system and the largest banks are heavily oriented towards their home regions. Every region, town, and often village has its own, made viable by protectionism and the highest savings rate in Europe. Banking services from funds transfer to medium-term loans is fragmented, esoteric and complicated.

Business organisation and structure

Regulation of business is minimal and, where it exists, open to manipulation. Italians created the art of accountancy in the fifteenth century and have been creative with it ever since. Independent outside audit for companies quoted on the stock exchange has only been a legal requirement since 1975. Independent auditors should not be confused with statutory auditors of joint stock companies who, on behalf of the directors, report to the shareholders that accounts follow a prescribed format. They have no powers to verify that they conform with the books of the company. Accounts of smaller private, unquoted firms should be treated with circumspection, remembering that their primary purpose is not to provide a full and fair picture to shareholders but to form a basis of negotiation with banks and tax authorities.

The board of directors (*consiglio d'amministrazione*) is headed by a *Presidente*. Under him there is usually a managing director (*Amministratore Delegato*). *Direttori* are department heads. Other titles, whether functional or status, are meaningless. If there is an organisation chart it will have been drawn up for a purpose other than clarifying the organisation, showing to foreign business partners perhaps.

In large companies a conventional hierarchy in the sense of clear reporting lines from superior to subordinate is only to be found at the lower levels of organisation. At middle to upper levels the true hierarchies are built on personal alliances between people in different parts of the organisation who trust each other and rely on each other to get things done. People have the power to influence and decide outside the apparent organisational structure. Finding the decision maker is an art, especially in a subsidiary of a holding company, where he may be in a different part of the organisation.

In public and private sectors, conglomerates are heavily decentralised. Within the same holding company there is a wide diversity of management styles among individual subsidiaries. The age and education of senior management and the age, size, technology and market of the companies determine how they are run. The key word in describing the Italian approach and the primary attribute demanded of a manager is 'flexible'.

Flexibility means ignoring procedures as part of the routine. Protocols, rules and organisation charts may well be drawn up and defined but they will be ignored as a matter of principle as well as practice. If there is a regulation it will be broken even if the breaking is more trouble than going along with it. Making sure that things are done properly and well is a question of personal supervision and trust in the competence and reliability of individuals. These key elements of control and trust are easier to ensure in paternalistic family companies than large corporations.

The disorganisation apparent to someone from a more systematic background is, in the highly competitive private sector at least, illusory. For these companies 'flexibility' means concentrating on what is essential to get a job done without getting bogged down in principle. Pragmatism and a talent for improvisation are more than a substitute for orthodoxy.

Planning

There is rarely a written strategic plan. It may be in the minds of the owner or the senior decision makers but it is unlikely to be promulgated. If it is written there is a purpose other than planning behind it. There is a strong temperamental aversion to forecasting and planning, especially to grandiose schemes on an industry or national level. At the same time there is a keen entrepreneurial sense based on recognition of new opportunities in the market. Italian companies thrive on ambiguity and risk. They will identify and exploit a niche without waiting for an in-depth analysis.

This can affect the quality of joint ventures with longer-term objectives. While alert to the opportunity of short-term gains there is a bias against long-term strategic positioning. A business association lasts only as long as it is consistently profitable.

Leadership

The traditional leadership model derives from the family company — the boss as autocratic father figure, the sons as senior managers with the ear and trust of the boss, the employees as faithful retainers who do as they are told and are well looked after. This works fine in family companies but is less effective when it is translated to a large and professionally managed organisation.

The single most important management issue I came across among Italians was the characteristics of effective leadership. It dominated all the conversations with Italians. (For non-Italians the predominant issue was the decision-making process.) For a number of reasons including technological demands, social pressures, economic pressures for larger business units, there was a strong feeling that traditional leadership styles are no longer appropriate. The head of a socialist cooperative, whose ideas on management were indistinguishable from the most ardent capitalist's, made a fine distinction between *autorita*, *autorevolezza* and *autoritarianismo* — authority, authoritativeness and authoritarianism. The distinction is important in any culture but vital in one in which impersonal organisational mechanisms have low credibility.

Authority derives ultimately from the owners of the firm and the chairman or the managing director who represent them. But it is not transmitted systematically through the organisation. It is delegated personally to individuals who can be trusted. Authority is attributed by employees to those whom they know have the personal confidence of the owner or senior manager. These do not necessarily have a corresponding place in the organisation. Title or position in the organisation is not necessarily a guide. For example a major marketing decision need not necessarily be made by the head of marketing, it may be taken by the boss with the company lawyer. Alternatively the head of the marketing department is not necessarily the one most qualified by training or experience in marketing but someone whom the managing director can work with best.

Authoritativeness is based as much on personal qualities as technical competence. Another manager in the public sector, this time a Christian Democrat, made a Catholic distinction between formal and substantive management behaviour. On a formal level the boss is expected to be simpatico, charismatic and creative and to demonstrate that he is the boss. He should make a *bella figura* as a manager as well as in other spheres of activity. On a substantive level, consistency and reliability were the traits most often mentioned. This is not to say that technical expertise counts for nothing. While role playing comes naturally to most Italians they are equally adept at sensing if there is a solid basis of competence behind the facade. The high quality of Italian engineering and design does not come from networking skills. The status of technical people, as opposed to finance or marketing, is consistently high.

Authoritarianism is the trap that Italian managers are most likely to fall into when they leave the environment of the small family company. To behave in a rough, dictatorial way, to expect and exact deference, is a common enough role model in small businesses where relationships are close. But it does not work among subordinates who have a purely utilitarian relationship with the company. They do not feel obliged to cooperate simply because of their position in the organisation or because it is written down in their contract of employment.

The most important part of the leadership role is not planning or decision making but implementation and control. To attempt to achieve either with clear instructions and procedures alone may lead to disappointment. Italians generally feel they can do the job better than their bosses and do not readily take instructions unless they feel a personal commitment to what they have to do. It is essential to achieve a consensus first and to obtain the commitment of people who are expected to carry out a task, otherwise it will not get done. It is not enough to get a verbal agreement that may be given out of politeness. Persuasion, insistence and follow-up are essential. But once it is obtained the energy, flair and creativity applied to executing it will be extraordinary.

Delegation

Delegation is on the basis of giving responsibility to trusted individuals. It is rarely defined in terms of goals or account-abilities which are often imprecise. This extends to job descriptions. Where they have been instituted they are for the record only and are usually put away in a desk and forgotten. People may be appraised by their bosses and notes put on the personal file but it is rare that they will be shown to, or discussed with, the individual concerned. Formal personal appraisal is very difficult for either side to manage, as is any direct criticism, unless it is in the context of a recognised personal relationship. The informal 'godfather' relationship, which some American companies attempt to institutionalise, is common in Italian companies and part of the informal hierarchy system.

Formal control systems concentrate on essential and prag-matic indicators, such as turnover, cashflow and gross profit, and are rigorously monitored. More subtle MIS systems, full of allocations and ratios, are usually seen as time wasting even if the systems are in place to deliver the information.

Teamwork and competition

Italian business relationships are based on mutual dependence and a sense of mutual obligation most easily satisfied with members of the extended family. The most successful organisations in Italy are the family or those modelled on the family. A purely salary based, contractual relationship is not enough; it does not create the right bond. It has to be in the context of a relationship based on honour.

Once a relationship has been established, based on a common purpose where everyone will visibly profit, there will be total cooperation and commitment. If the relationship has not been created colleagues will be highly competitive to the point of undermining each other.

For a team to work well it should have a respected leader capable of managing personal relationships. Teams composed solely of peers are difficult to maintain as there is no concept of power being shared equally by a group.

Meetings

Any process of open decision making is illusory. Decisions taken and agreed in formal meetings, minuted and scheduled for implementation may never happen. Meanwhile a different decision has been taken by someone else and implemented by his subordinates and allies.

They are usually unstructured and informal. The smaller the meeting the more unstructured it is. They may start with three or four people, a few more may come in, a few may go. It may not always be clear why some of them are there at all. Sometimes it feels like they are merely social gatherings to reinforce a sense of togetherness. You may get the impression that nothing is happening or a dozen things all at once. The purpose of meetings is to enable the decision takers to evaluate the mood of the others, to sense supporters and test the water, not usually to make decisions.

It is difficult to impose an agenda although it is always worthwhile trying if you are in a position to do so. Otherwise discussion may be interminable. There is a tendency to overanalyse and split hairs — *spaccare il capello in quattro*. A large proportion end without a satisfactory conclusion in which case they are always reconvened.

A meeting is often a stage for exhibiting eloquence,

personality and status and is consequently a free-for-all of opinions, comment and ideas. Everyone is entitled to make a contribution, is listened to and apparently agreed with. The weight of the idea resides not in the idea itself but in the importance and influence of the speaker. Newcomers or junior people will be paid the courtesy of a hearing, their contribution welcomed and accepted. But somehow their contribution gets left out at the end.

If a proposal is to be put to a meeting it is often advisable to clear it with each of the participants beforehand. Then they will react constructively. If a new idea is sprung on a meeting everyone will automatically object.

Opinions must not be imposed but agreed to. Making a decision on a vote is rarely a good tactic unless you know it will be unanimous. While people will not publicly go out on a limb to fight for a minority view, they will not submit to a majority decision. They will abandon the group or undermine its work from the inside. The guiding principle is not to offend the *dignita* of a dissident, but give him or her time to change opinion and to save face. If there are signs of entrenched positions the skilled chair will often adjourn the meeting. When it is reconvened, after some subtle lobbying, the objections will have disappeared.

Communication

Communication channels are tortuous and complicated. Informal contacts are vital in every aspect of Italian life and information is one of the ingredients. There is never a shortage of opinion but facts are usually in short supply. They are secretively guarded and traded on a transactional basis. The word *dietrologia* sums up the belief that behind every event there are sinister, powerful personalities or organisations, manipulating everything. The simple explanation is that because there is less emphasis on making clear goals and targets, companies are less transparent. Things get done without apparent reason, others die silently and nobody seems to know why.

If the telephone worked better it would be even more extensively used. It is mainly for fixing up and preparing the ground for personal meetings which are the main channel of communication inside or outside the company.

Formal presentations are not common in the Italian business environment and if called upon to make one an Italian may be uncharacteristically pompous and professorial unless he has an American training, in which case he may include even the obligatory laboured jokes.

Upward mobility

Relatives, connections, influence, membership of the right political party were, until recently, important considerations in making a career. In the British Social Attitudes Special International Report (1989), Italians were reported as believing that the most important factors in getting ahead were education, knowing the right people, ability, hard work and political connections. Ambition came sixth, lower than in the other countries surveyed. The thrusting, high flyer is more a figure of fun than a role model.

But, while being a cousin or *raccomendato* by a politician may get you on the bottom rung, it will not necessarily get you much further up the ladder. There is a strong and growing professional managerial class in the private sector. It is especially active in private companies which have outgrown their original family based structures. Thirty years ago a talented graduate would go into the public sector. Now the status, pay and opportunities are in the private sector even for a person with no direct connections.

There is no recognised educational élite although many managers in larger companies are graduates of the business school at Luigi Bocconi University. In the last ten years or so several other business schools and faculties have been set up.

There is a strong degree of company loyalty based on being closely acquainted with a group of people. Job security is important, reinforced by the difficulty in firing people. There is little job-hopping except among foreign multinationals. If there is a fast track it is based on nepotism. There is not yet the breed of professional manager who moves from company to company and those who do may find themselves squeezed out.

Attitudes and behaviour

Italians display an intense rectitude and loyalty in personal relationships, especially with family but also with anyone else who comes into the private sphere. It is paralleled by what outsiders may regard as amorality in relationships with institutions. Other companies, other departments, the government, banks, and their representatives are fair game, not necessarily for sharp practice but for arm's length transaction which outsiders may regard as unethical by their standards. By Italian standards ethics principally apply to personal relationships in which they are scrupulous, the inverse of cultures where civic responsibility outweighs personal morality.

They are receptive to fresh ideas, new solutions. Inventiveness and imagination are prized. They have a talent for improvising solutions — *pensiamo al remedio*. They will willingly cooperate with others as long as they get a chance to demonstrate their own skills.

To describe someone as *un tipo furbo* is not a compliment. It means sharp. It is much better to be *ingamba*, smart. At the same time it is important to demonstrate intelligence and education. Being cultivated is not a social grace but a social necessity. In researching this book the the most mundane of conversations about business were peppered with references to sources ranging from Aristotle to Umberto Eco, Adam Smith to JK Galbraith. At first such name dropping may seem pretentious to those from backgrounds where familiarity with literature and the classics is considered unbusinesslike.

Women

Social pressures on women to stay at home are, according to

the Eurobarometer survey of 1987, less than in many other EC countries. Despite maternity leave and favourable child care provision only 38 per cent of women under 65 are active in the official labour market, less than Britain with 61 per cent and Germany with 43 per cent. The proportion is made up by the 'black' economy.

Although there are some very successful individual business-women, there are very few women in managerial positions and few in the professions. The exception is in family companies where their status as family members outweighs their sex.

There is no more perceptible male chauvinism in Italy than in other countries with a greater proportion of women in positions of responsibility. But there is considerably less feminism.

Etiquette

Etiquette is based on an easy formality in which considerateness is more important than formulas. Whatever the relationship and whatever the rank and social class courtesy is important and good manners are prized.

The polite third person, the *lei* form, predominates, especially with senior people or in companies with a strong sense of hierarchy, for example most public sector organisations. The informal *tu* will only be used where there is a relationship based on something more than a business association. In newer companies with an open style of management, small family firms and among younger people, colleagues use first names and very quickly get to the *tu* form. Even then you will often probably call the boss and older colleagues *lei*.

If the lei form is used then last names will be the rule with *Signor* or *Signora*. *Signorina* is for young and junior women but *Signora* is the safest. Professional titles, most commonly *Dottore*, are often used. Dottore is used for any form of graduate and it will not be taken amiss if wrongly used. However there is no sense of stiffness or exclusion. Italians are very open people, curious and tolerant of other ways and other manners. If you are late, for example, it will not be held against you as long as you are genuinely apologetic. There is a high tolerance of inefficiency and genuine mistakes but a low tolerance of arrogance or rudeness.

People dress formally for business. Making a good impression matters deeply. The excellence of Italian taste and design are an expression of the Italian desire to make a *'bella figura'*. This is not superficial. It extends to social graces and courtesies, the kind of conversation you make, the kind of person you are.

It is not done to throw your weight around but it does not pay to be modest and retiring either. Be dignified but do not stand on dignity, authoritative but not authoritarian. The further North, the more seriously and soberly one behaves.

Punctuality

The attitude to punctuality is often misunderstood by meticulous northerners. Deliberate lateness is seen as sloppy. Taking others for granted by keeping them waiting is rude. Twenty minutes is about the limit of acceptability — after that there must be a good reason and an apology.

Nevertheless time is an artificial framework designed to get people more or less at the same time in the same place but ranks lower in priority than what you do inside the framework. If something intervenes to make you late, a meeting running over time, or a surprise visit from someone important, or an unexpected telephone call then it is understandable. While it is impolite to arrive late for a meeting it is even more impolite to break off the previous one because it is overrunning. If the appointment is more important than anything else, everyone will be meticulously on time.

In these circumstances an ability to juggle each other's appointment schedule is second nature. You are equally likely to be invited in to the tail end of a host's previous appointment as to be kept waiting outside. If the ensuing conversation is promising the two meetings may be rolled into one, someone else steps in and you all end up going out to lunch together. The end result is not in the timetable but may be more useful than anticipated.

Humour

Italians value wit, humour, and good spirits. It is important to enjoy life and work. Work should not be a burden or taken too seriously. They do not often tell jokes as such, with the exception of political ones. They are fond of irony and the humour of the incongruous. They can be self deprecating and there is a lot of good humoured banter.

At the same time they will be very aware of public dignity. When playing the institutional role, especially in public, the tone will change to formality and seriousness.

Socialising

The long lunch hour is common only in the South, where people are able to get home. In the urbanised North a nine-to-six routine is now the norm with a brief snack at noon. Large companies provide some sort of canteen facility or luncheon vouchers as a fringe benefit.

There is no recognisable pattern about socialising during or after work, no customary happy hour or drink in the pub after work. Groups of people will have parties and celebrations, including leaving parties, which will include people at all levels of seniority. Everyone is very approachable and there is no standing on ceremony.

Outside immediate working hours there is very little mixing. There is a sharp differentiation between work and private life. Taking work home, being telephoned at home or on holiday is unusual. Spouses are rarely involved in entertaining either at home, or at restaurants, and will rarely meet other colleague's spouses.

Drinking without eating, other than an aperitif at a cafe, is rare. Even mild intoxication is ill mannered. The hard drinking executive is a rarity. The usual form of entertainment is dinner in a restaurant. This is primarily a social not a business event, to find out if you each think the other the kind of person you wish to know. Those readers whose eyes glaze over when they are expected to talk shop after seven in the evening will find this to their liking. Those who believe that social occasions are an extension of the business day and like to talk about it on every possible occasion will find they get fewer and fewer opportunities to do so.

NETHERLANDS

'God created the earth but the Dutch made the Netherlands'. Twenty per cent of the country has been reclaimed from the sea and the process continues. The entire landscape, urban and rural, is an artefact designed to accommodate the most congested population in Europe. It is the most obvious manifestation of the Dutch belief that everything, whether land or society or business, can be moulded by human aspiration and reason and effort. At the same time there is an admission that dykes and societies and wealth are subject to external forces which have to be respected. You cannot afford to take chances with nature, physical or human.

So there are several aspects of the Dutch. One is a willingness to innovate and experiment, sometimes on a massive scale — the sheer nerve of blocking off what was the Zuider Zee, now known as the IJsselmeer. There is a sense that the world is their oyster, not only because they are a small country bursting at the seams, but that it is there for the taking with intelligence and courage. This is the Netherlands of enormous multinationals, technology based agriculture, enlightened experiments in illegal drug control and penal reform.

Another strain, at first sight contradictory, is deep conservatism. You must innovate and be bold to survive but at the same time minimise risk. Changing for its own sake or change that has not been thought through is to be avoided. The boy with his finger in the dyke is a symbol of failure as well as heroism — what happened to the safety margin? This is the bourgeois Netherlands of straight streets and clean windows, order and conformism.

The values of the Dutch are predominantly egalitarian rather than aristocratic, rural rather than urban. Independence and self-reliance are associated with an outward-looking and entrepreneurial maritime tradition. At the same time, physical proximity and the need for total cooperation in the management of limited resources have created a social system based on negotiated interdependence.

Regionalism

Holland is a region and not a synonym of the Netherlands. While the Dutch accept the confusion among tourists the country should be referred to by its correct name. Despite the size of the country and its density of inhabitants they draw clear distinctions between different regions, *gezellig* (affable) Brabant, for example, or cheese-eating Friesland, which has its own language. To an outsider the most noticeable difference is between the Randstad and the rest. The Randstad, or 'city on the edge', is the flat and sprawling conurbation between Amsterdam and Rotterdam, the Hague and Utrecht. This is the home of the entrepreneurial, hard-headed, maritime Dutch, of industry and ports and intensive agribusiness. The rest of the country, including the rolling and wooded hinterland, is more rural and traditional, less obviously dedicated to the relentless pursuit of wealth. However attached the Dutch are to their home region they are united in a fierce nationalism centred on the monarchy.

The principle divisions in the country are not by geography but by religion. The original provinces of the Low Countries that achieved independence from Spain in the seventeenth century parted company because of conflict between Catholics and Calvinists. The Catholic part broke away in 1830 to form what is now Belgium. But Protestant Netherlands under the House of Orange retained a large proportion of Catholics in the south. The two persuasions have arrived at an exemplary accommodation, assisted by the particular style of Dutch Catholicism which, to an outside observer, appears to genuflect as much to

68

Geneva as to Rome. A third group, the Liberals, is non-denominational. So there have been three versions of many political and social institutions, Catholic, Protestant and Liberal, from political parties to labour unions and social clubs. In recent years the groups have reformed on a political level into Christian, Liberal and Socialist but social clubs, education and so on still tend to be organised along traditional lines.

Sectarianism and discrimination are not serious issues. Tolerance and openness are active social and civic virtues. The relationship between the elements of society is characterised by dialogue and a search for accommodation based on what the Dutch call 'columnisation'. This does not mean consensus. Society is thought of as consisting of various columns or pillars each maintaining their own identity and values and supremely confident of their superiority over the others. Co-existence and not integration is the glue which holds society together. It is an approach which marks all spheres of life including business. A partnership with a Dutch company will tend to work better as a marriage of convenience between independent entities than a total merger.

Coalition of disparate interests is the dominant feature of political life. There are fourteen parties which mix and match to form the government. In the free spending seventies, when discoveries of natural gas financed a proliferation of welfare services, the balance teetered to the left. Now a right-of-centre coalition is restoring the balance with deregulation and privatisation. But the process cannot be described as confrontational or divisive, as in other countries which are carrying out a similar readjustment.

Internationalism

The Dutch, along with the Belgians, have the most open economies in Europe. Imports and exports each account for 60 per cent of GNP. Half of Europe's truck fleet is owned by the Dutch. They are a maritime, colonial and trading nation forced to make a living from a tiny base with no natural resources, at least until natural gas was discovered. There is another factor too. The Netherlands is Germany's entrepôt at the mouth of the Rhine, its window on the outside world. The Dutch economy rises and falls with the German, the guilder with the Deutschmark.

It is an economy of traders and middlemen, adding value to imported raw materials and re-exporting it again. A good example of this is the thriving and entrepreneurial agricultural sector which accounts for 20 per cent of exports. How does a small, urban, crowded country find the land and the resources to be the world's largest exporter of poultry and dairy products? To be the largest exporter of house plants and flowers? By importing feed, manufacturing fertilizer and forcing produce with cheap energy from natural gas. In Dutch agriculture 'organic' refers to the chemistry not the food.

The probability, therefore, of being in partnership with a Dutchman is as great as with businessmen from much larger countries. Dutch investment in the USA is the third largest after the UK and Germany. They rank fourth in the EC in the number of companies involved in acquisitions in 1989.

Foreign investment in the Netherlands is encouraged with considerable subsidy and incentives but these are by no means its only advantages. Other than tiny Luxembourg the Dutch are the most multilingual people in the EC and have an international outlook to match. A frequent strategy for companies wishing to exploit the single market is to acquire a Dutch company and let them get on with it.

Business environment

To the rest of the world Dutch business is typified by the great multinationals, Philips, Unilever, Royal Dutch Shell, and, for the connoisseurs, Akzo. These four, plus DSM which exploits the brown coal deposits of the north, employ 25 per cent of the labour force. Philips alone accounts for 9 per cent. But they are typical only of each other and of other major multinationals, not of the rest of industry which consists of small and medium sized privately owned enterprises.

In the past the state has played a direct part in industry

through strategic holdings in large companies such as Fokker and DAF. The present government's policy is to reduce the drain on the public purse and increase efficiency by privatisation. It is also seeking to reduce the burden on the private sector of the extensive welfare system, increasingly regarded as a brake on economic development. Frugal to the point of parsimony in their private and business affairs, the Dutch have been profligate in public spending. Natural gas has proved to be a mixed blessing in fostering consumption and, as a proportion of GNP, financing the highest welfare expenditure in Europe. While this has pushed the Netherlands to the forefront in the care of the disadvantaged it has created difficulties in the economy. Cutting the corporatist state down to size is the main concern of the present centre-right coalition government. A personal tax rate has recently been reduced from 72 per cent to 60 per cent and corporate tax from 42 per cent to 38 per cent

People from countries where the fiscal relationship between the state and individuals or corporations is adversarial should be aware that in the Netherlands it is generally above board. Tax avoidance is highly developed and there is a growing grey market, especially in the private building industry, but outright evasion is considered reprehensible and extremely risky.

The pillars of the business establishment are the banks. They are being deregulated to meet European standards of financial market liberalisation. They already have a universal role, acting as investment, commercial and merchant banks. They are directly represented on the stock exchange where they have predominant influence on the German model. While competing strongly among themselves, they tend to close ranks against foreign predators. Hostile corporate takeovers are extremely rare.

Industrial relations

The Netherlands has the highest rate of unemployment in Europe after Ireland and Spain. Some would say this has been encouraged by an over-generous welfare system and point to high levels of vacancies and labour shortages in lower paid occupations. Other factors are a high national minimum wage, the growing number of women in the labour market, sluggish industrial investment and the structural changes experienced by other post-industrial economies.

There are three main union groups, the Protestant CNV, the Catholic NKV and the Liberal NVV. They represent about 40 per cent of the workforce on an industry basis. They negotiate with the two employers' associations, the predominant non-denominational VNO and the joint Protestant-Catholic NCW. The latter work very closely together. Both sides sit together on a Joint Industrial Labour Council and with government representatives and independent experts on a Social and Economic Council. Until recently wage negotiations were at this national level and followed a cumbersome procedure. The government has begun to dismantle the structure in favour of local negotiations, which have become more aggressive. Strikes, while still rare, are more common than ten years ago. In general, however, industrial relations remain non-confrontational, based on negotiation and debate.

At the individual company level those which employ more than 35 people must set up a works council, *ondernemingsrad*. This is entitled to receive financial information, plans and forecasts, to be consulted on major changes such as investment and merger, and all aspects of personnel policy. Otherwise the employees have to be given the opportunity to question the management board at least twice a year.

Business organisation

The two most common sorts of company are NV, *Naamloze Vennootschapp*, a public limited company and BV, *Beslote Vennootschapp*, a private limited company. Both have to have a management board and a managing director. In addition a 'large' company must have a supervisory board of at least three people. A large company is defined by its capital and whether it has 100 or more employees in the Netherlands. Shareholders, works councils and the management board can nominate candidates and the first two have a right of veto. The supervisory board members, *Commissarissen*, cannot be employed by the company. Their job is to approve the strategic direction, appoint the management board, finalise the annual accounts and ratify major management decisions.

The supervisory boards have many powers which in countries like the USA or the UK are vested in the shareholders. There is strong protection for managers against shareholder interference. Decisions on mergers and acquisitions lie with the board rather than the shareholders. The Dutch manager of an independent company feels a lot more secure than his counterpart in other takeover-happy countries.

The Dutch countryside was described by an English writer, Aldous Huxley, as a rationalist's paradise, 'like a tour through the first books of Euclid'. There is a rationalist's aversion to the non-essential, an approach which permeates all aspects of social and organisational life. A Dutch organisation aspires to a rigorous system which, more importantly, is respected and adhered to by all its members. They are not obsessive legislators. There are right and wrong ways of doing things but only the essentials have to be codified into procedures. These are taken very seriously.

The Dutch are frugal, careful with money as individuals and companies, if not as governments. Organisations are lean and practical. There is a strong belief that the main function of business is to make profits. The bottom line is paramount. At the same time they are not obsessed with numbers. A strategy has to be qualitatively and conceptually right and not quantified in detail, unlike the operating plan and profit reports.

The strategic orientation is made clear down to relatively low levels in the organisation. While there is a belief in hedging the unexpected by careful planning and study the plan is not characteristically a highly developed and numbers-based document. They avoid the grandiose in favour of cautious, pragmatic and step-by-step development. If reality does not conform to their projections they are prepared to improvise.

Leadership

Hierarchical systems are generally shallow and boundaries are flexible. People will cut across reporting lines if necessary. The egalitarianism and openness evident in society is reflected at the workplace. The Dutch are easily shocked by the hierarchical discrimination practised in many other cultures. Seniority is a necessary convenience and power is camouflaged rather than flouted. The boss is a *primus inter pares*, 'one of us'. He is therefore seen as the most important collaborator. This does not mean that he does not exert authority or is treated as one of the gang. He has usually grown up with the company and has not been brought in, either as a professional senior manager or a graduate high flier. The exception would be in smaller, more fluid high-tec companies.

Relationships between all levels are generally open and highly tolerant. Communication is open and transparent. There is a preference for *buurten*, which means 'visiting' in the American sense, over written communication. Dutch are not good at keeping secrets and uncomfortable with deviousness, their own as much as others'. Everyone is expected to make suggestions and contributions and expects his upward com-munications to be listened to with respect. At the same time they are conservative and resistant to change. While brain-storming and kicking ideas around in a group are perfectly feasible and nothing will be dismissed outright, ideas have to be well researched and thought out before they are taken seriously. There is a mistrust of intuition and a requirement for clarity.

Meetings

Meetings are regular and frequent and despite an informality of manner stick to the basic protocols of keeping to an agenda, speaking through the chair and so on. They are primarily for decision making after thorough discussion. While this is exhaustive it is usually concise and to the point. It is essential to come well prepared and not to utter ill-informed opinion, however scintillating. All members are expected to contribute, whatever their seniority and there is a strong sense that ideas are objective and independent of the people uttering them. The directness of comment might seem offensive to those from cultures where the quality of an idea is more closely identified with the identity of its begetter.

Individuals are held accountable for decisions but only after active consensus has been established. Every interested person has to be fully committed. Obedience is not an overriding virtue and people will not assent to a position unless they are convinced it is right. Vote-taking or any other formula which leaves a dissenting minority would be regarded as high-handed. It treads on individuals' rights to make themselves heard and to hold a different opinion. At the same time considerable pressure is put on dissenters to conform to a majority view and will persist until they have done so. The process is therefore slow and ponderous and, for some outsiders, frustrating. But once a decision is made implementation is fast and efficient because it has been thoroughly thought through and everyone knows what their role is.

Job descriptions tend to be oriented less towards tasks and targets than towards how an individual interrelates with colleagues. Cooperation and trust are valued higher than individual performance and all forms of one-upmanship are frowned upon. It is important to attribute success to the team and not to oneself or another individual. Conversely, there will be little blame or recrimination if things go wrong. It is important to avoid embarrassing other individuals. Overt cooperation does not, however, preclude covert rivalry and as much behind the scenes politicking as in more openly competitive societies.

It would be misleading if this gave the impression that the Dutch are obsessively collaborative and conciliatory in manner. They dislike being answerable to other individuals and to those from a more directive culture may appear unyielding and opinionated. They regard interference in what they regard as their sphere of responsibility as an infringement of trust.

Upward mobility

Dutch take a long term view of things, including their own careers. Innate conservatism includes a strong need for security. It is unusual to job hop. There is a great sense of company loyalty reinforced by the pension structures. Because pay agreements are highly standardised and collectivised there is not a lot of incentive to move for pay. Individual performance related pay would be against the collective ethos. If people do move it is early in their career, usually before the age of 30.

As reported in the British Social Attitudes International Report (1989), when asked to rank the factors influencing getting ahead in life the Dutch ranked education, hard work, ambition, ability and knowing the right people.

Progress through a Dutch company is slow and methodical. The scope for promotion is largely determined by educational background. There are not many shop floor to boardroom stories. Most of the senior people will have received a vocational education at the universities of Delft, specialising in engineering, Rotterdam, for Economics, and Leiden for law and the humanities. These are the basis of a powerful old-boy network. There is also an aristocracy, which forms a clubbish group mainly within the banks and the diplomatic service.

For the less exalted the apprenticeship system, along German lines, is still important. Further training tends to be on the job.

For such an egalitarian and socially responsible nation the Dutch are surprisingly chauvinistic about women in business. There are few in a managerial capacity. Women only began to come into the labour market in any numbers in the 70s. They account for about 30 per cent of the workforce. Married women tend to give up work for good when they have children and making a career is a rarity.

Attitudes and behaviour

Etiquette

The Dutch are so adept at dealing with foreigners that you will usually find that you are using your own etiquette. Among themselves they tend to combine a frank, no-nonsense informality of manner with strict observance of basic etiquette. Unless there is a large generation or seniority gap, colleagues at all levels will rapidly come to first name terms instead of *Meneer* or *Mevrouw* and use the informal singular form, *je*, rather than the polite *U*. Titles, like Doctor or Professor are sometimes used. If it is not apparent from the first introduction that the other person prefers you to use a title, it is not necessary to do so, even if it is on his business card. A very different standard applies to formal communication and especially letters. It is important to use the right titles and formulas and modes of address.

Dress is informal, the extent depending on the conventions of the industry. In some companies this may mean open-necked shirts and sweaters and unpolished brown shoes with a suit reserved for outside meetings and special occasions. In the *bourse* and banks they wear dark suits. In any event taking off the jacket means getting down to work. In some companies informality of dress, down to jeans and T-shirts, may be a privilege of seniority. The same double standard applies to dress on formal occasions as to letters. When the occasion demands proper dress, even to white tie and tails, the conventions are carefully adhered to.

Whatever style is current it is more important to avoid pretension and deviousness than a breach of formal manners. This includes self deprecation or diffidence. To be businesslike and straightforward to the point of bluntness is a greater mark of respect than ostentatious graciousness. To those used to hedging and hinting this can be disturbing at first.

They look for solid personal relationships based on inter-dependence and reliability, mutual respect and mutual profit. It is important to honour commitments, however trifling. There is much more importance attached to the spirit than the letter of agreements which, if they are written at all, are cursory. Schedules, routines and diaries are carefully structured and adhered to. Lateness, missed appointments, postponements, late delivery, are not merely inconvenient. To a Dutchman they mean untrustworthiness and will quickly sour a relationship. While a high value is placed on punctuality a compulsion to make productive use of every minute sometimes puts a strain on the timetable.

One of the few exceptions to directness is sometimes a reluctance among business partners to give a straight yes or no to a proposal. A concern to avoid conflict and a reluctance to postpone the definitive decision leads to phrases like 'let's take it a bit further' meaning yes, or 'this could produce problems' meaning no.

In accordance with the basic value of frugality, ostentation is to be avoided in all circumstances. While accumulating money is a virtue, spending it is a vice. Offices are simple, clothes are subdued, cars are modest, even the notepaper and letterhead are basic and unadorned. Those who put on style are considered not merely wasteful but suspect. Frequent mention of frugality and modesty perhaps gives a false impression that the Dutch are meek and dour. In most circumstances they are assertive and forceful and stubborn and extremely tough negotiators.

Humour

Speeches and formal presentations are frequently tinged with good humour but informal business discussions tend to remain serious. Humour is jocular and earthy rather than witty, while irony and sarcasm invariably backfire with a people who prize plain speaking. This literal approach to language favours humour based on logical absurdity and paradox. Given social sensitivities, it is wise to avoid jokes about religion.

Socialising

There is no tangible dividing line between formal and informal contacts, no sense of occasion about a monthly meeting or a conversation with the boss. There is not a rigid barrier between home and office. People will take work home and can be telephoned there on important matters.

Socialising takes place over coffee rather than meals. Food is not an important part of a social culture and the cuisine is not a source of pride. Meals are plain and private. Their place is within the family and not for social entertaining. Lunch is a necessity not an event and a sandwich at the desk is the norm. The works canteen, if there is one, is for workers. The business lunch is often perfunctory although there is a growing trend to eat at restaurants. Business entertaining is regarded as a personal occasion and not corporate entertainment.

Social occasions at work include staff parties at St Nicholas — the festive element of Christmas — and other times during the year. Birthdays are celebrated with cakes and coffee. Colleagues may mix socially at weekends or evenings if they are neighbours but not immediately after work. People go home promptly and eat dinner early with their family. Entertaining colleagues or business partners at home is not common and it is more usual to be invited after dinner rather than for dinner. This should not be taken as a sign of a lack of hospitality and it is advisable not to eat much beforehand. Guests are plied with plentiful snacks and sandwiches along with drinks and the inevitable coffee but the indulgence and slight embarrassment of a formal meal are avoided.

SPAIN

The new Spain

In the past ten years or so old Catholic Spain, dominated from Madrid, its face turned away from Europe to Africa and its old colonies in the New World, dominated by church and state and bankers and bureaucrats and old families who counted their names, has been pushed aside. It has by no means disappeared but is inhabited by a superannuated generation bewildered by change.

The collapse of traditional authority systems of family, church and state, the transition to a pluralist democracy, membership of the EC, economic deregulation, a wave of foreign investment seeking to exploit cheap labour and the fifth largest market in Europe, have opened the floodgates to a young generation anxious to rebuild a European Spain.

Whether one believes it is for the better or the worse, the change is striking. While impoverished gentility was the hallmark of the middle classes, making money has now become fashionable. Business is glamorous. Footballers and bullfighters now share the covers of popular magazines with young millionaires. An active and growing stock exchange, a thriving property market, industrial investment and rampant consumerism have created a breed of entrepreneur previously unknown. A younger generation who left Spain for travel and study are more ambitious and less cautious than their parents who learned to be defensive and careful under the old régime.

Regionalism

With the benefit of hindsight it is obvious that the new Spain was there all the time, a sub-culture beneath the surface of Francoism. The political fragmentation that has occurred in the past 15 years has its roots in an older Spain. A quarter of Spaniards speak a language in addition to, or instead of, Spanish, the language of Castile. The most important are Basque, Galego (the language of Galicia similar to Portuguese) and Catalan — languages in their own right and widely spoken in their home territory. The Civil War was fought as much over separatism as socialism. The aspirations for autonomy of Catalans, Galicians and above all Basques was ruthlessly driven underground. It resurfaced before the ink was dry on the 1978 Constitution, which established a system based on Autonomous Communities.

It was not only the above three *nacionalidades historicas* which achieved self government. Fourteen others claimed it or had it thrust upon them with varying degrees of enthusiasm. There are now 17 regions each with its own capital, flag and legislature. Their responsibility and powers and, for Spaniards the most important, their authority to raise taxes, varies. Basques collect their own taxes, control their own police, have their own television channel, run their own schools. Others are independent from Madrid virtually in name only.

Euskadi, or the Basque Region, is probably the best known of the *nacionalidades historicas* outside Spain through the activities of ETA, its independence movement. Like the IRA in Britain, its activities affect not only its immediate region but subvert the integrity of national politics and state institutions. Euskadi's economic importance lies in the iron and steelworks of Bilbao, once the wealthiest part of Spain but now the victim of the same blight that affects most other European centres of heavy industry — disinvestment, pollution and outdated technology.

Galicia is less well known to European businessmen and will probably remain so. Green, wet and windswept in its Atlantic climate it is reminiscent of Ireland, not least in its economic backwardness and high emigration rate. Catalonia is the most

81

thriving of the three. It has managed to retain its individual character despite the large number of immigrants from the rest of Spain attracted by its economic prosperity. Barcelona thinks of itself as more cosmopolitan, forward looking and industrious than the rest of Spain.

Southern Spain is in sharp contrast with these northern regions. Andalusia is the Spain of Flamenco and Moorish arches and more concerned with the quality of life than their earnest and solid northern compatriots. The inhabitants of Murcia, next door, have a similarly unfair reputation in the rest of Spain as those of the mezzogiorno in Italy, idle when they are at home and cheap labour when they are not. The Spain of Don Quixote — Castile, La Mancha and impoverished Estramadura — share the vast, high, arid central plain between North and South. Madrid is in the middle, an island of prosperity aloof from the surrounding areas. The popular *hidalgo* image of Spaniards as superior and reserved derives more from Castilian manners than the relaxed and unpretentious style of the rest of Spain.

Despite regional loyalties, economic circumstances foster a high migration rate both externally and internally. Yet companies who need to transfer employees between regions are careful about local sensibilities.

Attitude to government

Since the first referendum in 1976 Spaniards have gone to the polls over forty times. The excitement of the early years is beginning to wear thin. The turmoil has resulted in a remarkable continuity and stability of government oriented around the centre left PSOE party of Felipe Gonzales. Extreme right and left wing interests, feared in the early years of democracy, have been marginalised.

The landslide of elections and a new breed of more representative legislators has not enhanced, in many Spanish eyes, the credibility or competence or honesty of government. There is as much deep mistrust of officialdom as ever. That regional government brings the administrators closer to their constituents has not made them any better disposed towards it, especially as taxes have increased to finance it. Two-tier government means two pairs of hands in the till.

Attitudes to government, especially in respect of taxes, are sometimes explained, as in Italy and Greece, as a hangover from days when the government was an occupying power. In Spain's case, especially if you were a Catalan or a Basque, the alien power was Madrid. The argument seems pretty tenuous in a democratic society that elects its own government. There is a deeper reason, to do with a conception of what constitutes a community. In Spain and other Mediterranean countries a community is based on personal and family ties. What may appear to be favouritism and corruption is the exercise of mutual obligations. In the less family oriented countries of northern Europe it is based on a more abstract idea of common interest. Whether this derives from accidents of geography or climate or history or anything else is open to debate. The fact remains that foreigners used to an equitable relationship between governors and governed should be prepared for a different attitude to the authorities.

State intervention

The direct participation of government in the economy is pervasive both through direct holdings and the state holding company INI, Instituto Nacional de Industria. INI dominates the three major industries which have been the traditional back-bone of the economy, iron and steel, shipbuilding and textiles as well as a large number of other sectors including the airline Iberia. Many of its companies are in the lame duck category.

The business élite of Spain are the bankers. Until the recent reforming and restructuring of the stock exchange banks were the sole source of long- and short-term finance to the private sector. They will remain the dominant source for the conceivable future.

Although many banks belong to industrial groupings and have direct shareholdings in companies, there is no concept of a 'house' bank. Because of lending limits, to guard against fickle withdrawing of credit and to maintain secrecy, a company will usually have as many banks as it can. It will divulge as little information about its financial situation as possible. As a result bank lending is rarely unsecured.

Private sector

The profitable and well managed companies are mainly in the private sector. This is dominated by small family owned companies and foreign investors. Foreign investment plays a major role in the economy in providing not only finance and technology but management know-how in a country sorely lacking in professional skills. While most Spaniards recognise this and are receptive and open to foreigners, the welcome dissipates rapidly if they sense they are being patronised. They are looking for an equal partnership and not a client relationship.

The desire for a long-term business partnership works better on an individual than a corporate level. Few joint ventures have had lasting success. Wholly owned subsidiaries, either by establishment or acquisition have a better chance. Attitudes towards authority and leadership, discussed later on, create disagreements over control.

The accounting profession is still in a formative stage. There is no supervisory body in charge of pronouncing on generally accepted accounting principles. With the exception of quoted companies which are well regulated it is prudent to verify company accounts and all other financial information. Until recently there has been, effectively, only tax accounting rather than financial accounting. It should not be assumed that if the official books comply with tax law they present the actual financial situation and results of operations.

Rapid economic growth has created a serious skills shortage at all levels and especially managerial talent. Universities and vocational training schools have been making major efforts to develop business related courses and there has been a spate of new, private business schools. At least ten have been set up in the past two years. Since 1975 many young people have gone abroad for higher education, primarily to France. There is a major difference between the skills and approach by those whose formative years were spent in large bureaucratic companies and those who left Spain to make a career abroad before returning home.

A traditional style of Spanish management is found in family companies, large state-owned companies and some of the older established multinationals with Spanish senior management. They tend to be run on highly compartmentalised, bureaucratic and authoritarian lines. The introduction of, primarily, American management methods and the attitudes to authority among younger people brought up in the new political climate often generates conflict and stress between generations.

Business organisation and structure

There are two forms of company. The stock company, *Sociedad Anonima* (SA) and the *Sociedad de Responsabilidad Limitada* (SRL). They can have as few as one director. Companies with more than 500 employees and two directors must have an employee representative on the board. Those with over 50 employees have to have a works committee.

Traditional Spanish organisations are built on the concept of personal hierarchy. An organisation chart, if there is one, is a social rather than a functional system. Companies are run by instruction from the top passing down a recognised chain of command. The purpose of demarcation is not to enhance operational efficiency by a division of labour, but to enhance control by senior management. The concept of a team, if it exists at all, is one of individuals working independently under a strong leader. One chief executive I talked to was proud that his departments did not communicate with each other. This meant that they could not interfere in each other's work.

There is a strong sense of order and discipline which is practical and tangible rather than theoretical. Rules, systems, mechanisms are seen as a last resort to stop things falling apart. The reluctance to trust in systems means that there is a constant atmosphere of crisis and emergency. To be good at coping with it is a source of pride and felt to be a lot more enjoyable than being a cog in a machine.

The centralisation of the old Spain created an organisational model to match. In state owned companies, run like the ministries which control them, and large private companies there is an elaborate organisational framework bound together by tentacular documentary procedures whose ultimate purpose has long disappeared from view. This is rapidly changing in the burgeoning private sector. Organisational methods based on decentralisation, target setting and functional specialisation are fast taking root, creating a serious generation gap between younger and older managers over 50.

Planning

Forecasting and planning is not a salient feature of Spanish business practice. Who knows what will happen tomorrow? It is partly a question of mentality and partly because the mechanisms for forward planning are underdeveloped. In an environment where accounting for yesterday is rudimentary, accounting for tomorrow is a luxury.

Fixing a strategy is the responsibility of the chief executive or the owner. It will be based on intuition and business sense rather than systematic study. If it is communicated at all, which no-one expects, it will be in the form of vague hints and admonitions. There is no taste for intellectual schemas and grand designs. The preference is for the tangible, the practical and the opinions of people one trusts. Time spent gathering numerical information and making studies is seen as time wasted. Information gathering is a question of talking to as many people as one can without letting on what you are trying to find out. In a business environment where numbers of any sort are unreliable or non-existent it is the only tactic.

In a more modern company, if there is a formal, written plan it is likely to have been put together by strategic planning consultants for the benefit of senior managers. But translating it into specific action plans may be beyond the experience or inclination of middle management.

A traditional family company is unlikely to have financial plans or budgets or accounts. The key numbers are turnover and cashflow. Unless they are declining other figures are unimportant. Sensitivity to the 'bottom line' in the sense of net profit is not highly developed. In many companies there are not yet the systems that are capable of showing it nor, if there are, a willingness by top management to share the information. Accounting systems are designed not to enlighten but to conceal financial information from tax authorities and banks.

This is rapidly changing under the influence of foreign investors and business partners who demand what they consider to be proper reporting. The stock market is also exerting pressure for accounting standards and independent auditing. Spanish investors have been wary of investing directly in companies and prefer to use the intermediary of investment funds which spread the risk and benefit from better intelligence than the individual can hope to get. But shareholders and entrepreneurs have woken up to the potential of a well regulated, independent and active market to raise capital and realise personal fortunes.

Leadership

The ideal leader is a benevolent autocrat. Outsiders who are used to a more participative style are best advised to reserve it until they have established themselves as firm and decisive. The quality most admired in a leader is to be courageous — *vaillente*. Sharing decision making with subordinates may be interpreted as weakness and is more likely to generate insecurity than commitment. If a subordinate has a problem he or she expects the boss to solve it, if a question, to know the answer. This by no means precludes explanation of decisions and seeking opinions and comment, especially among younger people, as long as it remains clear who is in charge.

Authority does not automatically go with status but is determined by the quality of personal relationship with subordinates. A rigid adherence to protocol, insistence on proper channels of authority and communication will alienate them. Loyalty is to people and not institutions.

As in most directive cultures the problem is not in making decisions. Lines of authority are clear and decisions are passed up the line until they stick. The problem is in getting a commitment to implementing them.

Delegation should be concrete and specific, based on realistic short-term targets and detailed instructions in how to reach them. The written job profile is an innovation, if it exists at all. Few large companies have them. Spanish employees of the old school might feel slighted if they were given written instructions. If they do exist they are a general list of responsibilities with little advice on how to get the job done.

Appraisal systems of any sort are rare. Spaniards are used to criticism in the sense of being reprimanded by the boss, the *jefe*, for something they have done or not done, without right of reply. This is expected. It is a privilege of the boss to assert authority. Criticism is an exercise of rank rather than a constructive or meaningful piece of feedback and the person reprimanded will certainly not admit that he or she is in the wrong. People are surprised by positive feedback and are not as anxious to know how they are doing as they are, say, in Anglo-Saxon cultures. It implies a dependency which they would rather not acknowledge. The presumption is they are doing fine and, if not, it is someone else's fault. A general review of performance, especially if it is backed up by objective fact, takes on a more personal tone and is resented. They also resent criticism by people with whom they have a more informal relationship. You can criticise a subordinate without mincing words but it is much more delicate to point out something to a colleague.

Control

Operating plans have the same status as forecasts and are usually not much better developed. Where they exist they are interpreted as instruments of control over individuals rather than blueprints for action. They will tend to be understated to minimise the chances of recrimination. Schedules, budgets, forecasts tend to be rough guides. Management information systems, especially in a production environment, are preponderantly couched in quantities — kilos, units of production, amounts delivered — rather than financial units. This makes the concept and the execution of quality hard to introduce. Delivery dates are often approximations not to be taken literally. Outsiders who believe that the installing of sophisticated reporting systems is a first step are correct as long as they realise it is not the last. Making it work by personal negotiation with the people responsible is the second.

One barrier to the enhancement of internal control and audit systems is that they are interpreted as a lack of trust, a personal slight. Large customers who try to impose detailed schedules and quality checks are resented. Suppliers have difficulty in persuading independent agents and dealers to conform to accounting and control systems.

Meetings and teams

Spanish like to be independent and make decisions on their own. It appeals to their sense of bravery. It is not a meetings culture. The traditional function of meetings, if they occur at all, is to communicate instructions. Managers who try to use them constructively complain that the necessary participative skills have still to be learned by people used to a closed and authoritarian society. With the wholesale introduction of predominantly American methods and philosophy, this has begun to change. Social and political developments too have affected the expectations of employees about their role within organisations. It is a duty to indulge in free speech. While individual accountability is still the basis of organisational life, automatic assumptions about authority are being questioned and participation increasingly demanded at all levels. This leads to frequent complaints by older style managers that meetings are too frequent, too long and too ineffective.

Spaniards may say they do not work well in meetings, or in teams generally, because they are individualist and 'jealous'.

There is certainly a streak of anarchism in Spanish mentality which is used to justify authoritarianism in many spheres of life. But it also derives from a conception that collaboration has more to do with voicing opinion than arriving at decisions or, still less, implementing them. This leads to a concept of the meeting as a forum to express ideas of which one will be chosen. A contribution to a debate is seen less to further the aim of the meeting than the personal goals of the person making it.

Participants are protective of their own idea, which they will be more inclined to defend than amend. The arbiter is regarded as the most senior person present. If he or she makes a proposal then the purpose of the meeting is to obtain agreement of the others to it. The idea that a meeting can be used to decide on an action plan, allocate responsibilities and coordinate implementation is a novelty. Those who are used to collaboration producing a result to which everyone has contributed something, and in which everyone shares responsibility, will find this frustrating. People will feel free to raise ideas and objections but in the end they feel it is the boss's neck that is on the line.

Unless the chairman constantly pulls the subject back to the matter in hand, the agenda, if there is one, will be rapidly abandoned. At the same time it is important to force the agreement out of others because they will criticise and undermine later on. It is not usually advisable to ratify a decision on a majority vote because the outvoted minority will feel slighted. Consensus is most easily reached by getting everyone to agree with the chair rather than with each other.

Communication

The need to communicate to subordinates or colleagues anything other than what is strictly necessary to do the job is an innovation. Management keeps a closed door, especially if they are talking to someone else. There is plenty of one-to-one communication with the boss, as this is the conventional way for decisions to be made and instructions given, while everyone else wonders what they are talking about. Except in the largest companies there is a marked absence of correspondence and memos and staff noticeboards. Communication is predominantly oral and, since the telephone system works so badly, face-to-face.

Upward mobility

Until the recent rapid expansion of the economy there was relatively little scope for ambition. It was not a success culture. People were content with the station or rank or job they thought they were entitled to and could do well. Job security was a more important consideration than advancement. This has changed, especially among the young in cities like Madrid and Barcelona. There is a shortage of skills and a consequent jobs merry-go-round, with no inhibitions about leaving for better pay. Consumerism, so long inhibited by economic stagnation, has created the incentive system that the rest of Europe has enjoyed for much longer.

However, people will not move to a different locality for promotion. The extended family is still the basic economic unit, source of security and social framework. Family ties prevail and migration is still a symptom of desperation not ambition. In all cities a regional accent is the mark of the labouring not the managerial class and an impediment to promotion.

Education is seen as the key to progress and there is a thirst for training of all kinds. Some foreign companies, in an attempt to get off the wages spiral, offer training or education subsidies as an incentive to prospective employees. There is as yet no educational élite. Some point to one or other of the Jesuit Universities or the Opus Dei University in Navarre. As for Opus Dei itself, as is the case with the Masonic order, or any other secret society, its practical influence in everyday business life is hard to gauge.

In many Spanish companies, family is still more important than intelligence in recruitment. Family connections will have gained access to the better Universities or paid for a foreign education if this was too demanding and guarantee an appropriate standard of breeding and manners.

Personal loyalty, friendship and ability, in that order, are the most important qualifications for promotion. Intelligence, in the sense of cleverness, is a quality that Spaniards rate lower than character and breeding. There is not the admiration of cleverness, sly quick-wittedness, that is implied in the Italian *ingamba* or the Greek *exipno*. *Listo* is the closest, meaning sharp and not altogether trustworthy. *Intelligente* implies solid and boring. *Bueno*, as in *un tipo bueno* is the best compliment. It implies being clever, honourable and *vaillente*.

Attitudes and behaviour

Competitiveness

While relationships are familiar or even jocular there is little sense of collegiality. Working relationships are vertical rather than horizontal. The word which was most used to decribe feelings about peers was not rivalry or competitiveness but jealousy. Success is generally viewed as a matter of good luck and influence rather than capability or performance. To have got ahead is probably because you have insinuated yourself with the boss or are related to him, not a result of effort. Promotion is more often seen as a step up to privilege and an easy life rather than greater responsibility.

The successful are expected to flaunt their achievement. In the puritan and impoverished dictatorship to be overtly successful was to invite unwelcome attention. In the euphoric expansion of the past decade it is highly desirable to be seen to be making good — a German car, an expensive house, good clothes, a retinue of assistants and secretaries and other hangers-on. The ultimate accolade is to feature in one of the new business magazines.

Women

In the 1987 Eurobarometer survey asking about the ideal role of women, 47 per cent thought that women should have equally demanding jobs as men and share domestic duties equally. This was third largest proportion after Denmark and the UK. At the same time 28 per cent thought that women should not have a job and stay at home, the fourth largest after Germany, Ireland and Luxembourg. So there is a significant polarisation of opinion.

Women have not made the inroads into the professions as they have in other male dominated societies. A woman lawyer is a rarity. Women managers have in the past been associated primarily with family owned companies where there is no male line but the large size of families has made this statistically unlikely. It is uncommon to find women at any level of the organisation making a career. They disappear from the job market in their 30s and do not reappear.

The skills shortage is the best hope for women to break into the male preserve of management. Women with professional qualifications are welcome and, according to both men and women, accepted in their own right. The problems come from unqualified men who feel threatened by technocrats of either sex. But educationally qualified women are a recent phenomenon. While they have made gains in the battle for acceptance at entry level, they have yet to test their potential for making a career.

Etiquette

Spanish business and social behaviour, in all but the most elevated circles, is very informal. Familiarity is a basic facet of Spanish life. You call the maid and the doorman *usted* and your colleagues and the boss *tu*. This is confusing for Latin Americans for whom it is the other way round. It is very important not to call your subordinates *usted* because that puts them on the same level as domestic staff. With everybody you get very quickly onto first name terms. In the South of Spain, where manners are slightly more formal than the North, it may take a little longer to get on *tu* terms.

In the office, at meetings, at restaurants, it is common to take off jackets and even loosen your tie. On a very formal occasion, or with strangers, or if there is a wide mix of ranks, it pays to be circumspect and see what the others do. Even then, manners are based on an easy and relaxed informality. Human relationships are very important. A good working environment does not mean nice surroundings but rewarding relationships with colleagues. The best reference you can give another person is, 'he is a good friend of mine'. It does not mean a penetration of the privacy barrier, as in Germany or the UK. It is an easy relationship based on trust deriving from a personal sense of honour, *orgoullio*, and reinforced by respect.

Modesty is valued over assertiveness. Demonstrating superiority or intelligence or ability is not highly valued. With people like Italians or French, to whom selling yourself forcefully, clearly and rationally is part of the game, they appear understated. With opinionated people like Germans and British, who try to give the impression that they know best, they may appear diffident or vacillating. When they speak a foreign language their understatement is exaggerated since often they are wary of being ridiculed for speaking it badly.

Spaniards feel a great sense of personal pride and honour. Anything that diminishes or impinges will spoil a relationship. But it is important to know what they are proud of. Technical ability, professionalism, competence does not concern a Spaniard as much as pride in personal qualities. What may sometimes be interpreted by outsiders as intolerance of other people's views is from their point of view a stong sense of self-reliance and personal worth.

Punctuality

Procrastination and delay are endemic. In the kind of business environment that readers of this book will be operating it would be wrong to associate this with indolence or obstructionism. Rather it is more likely to be attributable to an attempt to cram too many things into too short a time. The popular conception of the *mañana* attitude is to be found in the stifling bureaucracies of the state sector and not the bustling private firms.

Humour

In public or in formal situations senior people cultivate a serious and dignified image in which joking is out of place. On all other occasions it is important to be amusing and entertaining and good company in and out of the office. This does not imply that work is not taken seriously but that it is not necessary to be solemn about it. Humour is often bantering and personal but is not characteristically biting or sarcastic about other individuals and is not used as a weapon. Foreigners as a class or people from other regions are fair game. Catalans have sleepy Andalucian jokes and Andalucians have miserly Catalan jokes. Self-deprecating humour would be at odds with a strong sense of personal dignity and is rare.

Socialising

It is common for colleagues to have lunch together but not for ranks to mix. In any case senior people will be lunching with outsiders. Canteens are single status but the boss would rarely eat there. Social life outside work tends to be with people of the same level in different companies.

Lunches and dinners are a vital part of business life. They are used to establish a personal relationship, to see if the chemistry is right and that each can trust each other. This is done by discussing everything except business until coffee is served when the host will bring up the specific subject of the meeting. Until then one is not expected to bare one's soul nor to remain distant and formal. The strength of a business relationship depends less on a community of interest than a community of feeling.

UNITED KINGDOM

Regionalism

Those who refer to the citizens of the United Kingdom as the English rather than the British risk irritating citizens of Scotland, Wales and Northern Ireland. Scotland has its own legal and educational system and Edinburgh is a financial centre second to London, albeit some way behind. Wales finds its identity in language. In some rural areas Welsh is the first language, taught in schools and used on radio and television. Although British society and culture is essentially homogeneous, outsiders who work in these regions are advised to acknowledge the pride taken in what may appear to be superficial differences between them.

Northern Ireland's previous independence has been eroded by an inability to govern itself through sectarian discrimination and violence. Unless they are directly involved in business there it is unnecessary for outsiders to become any better informed about the problem than those on the mainland. Outside Northern Ireland religion plays little part in everyday life. In Britain 35 per cent of the population claim to have no religion, the second highest proportion in Europe after the Netherlands. Disinterest has created an atmosphere of religious freedom and tolerance.

The British population has long been characterised by internal and external migration. There is a constant drift to the more prosperous South. Out of a total population of 57 million, 47 million live in England. About a million people have emigrated over the past five years, almost exactly balanced by the number of immigrants, mainly from the Carribean and the Indian sub-continent.

Political and economic decision making and administration is highly centralised in London. The counties surrounding the capital are known as the home counties, as if the others were extraneous. The area within a couple of hours' drive from London is known as 'the South'. The rest of the country is known as 'the North'. The South is perceived by those who live there as superior in wealth, sophistication and social status. It owes its image to the preponderance of service, high tec and other growth industries while the North is associated with heavy industry, engineering, mining and unemployment.

The United Kingdom is an urban society. A fifth of the population of mainland Britain lives in eight cities, the largest being London with almost seven million inhabitants. There is a wide spread of living standards from some of the worst slums in Europe to the affluent estates of the South. In London only the very rich or the very poor live in the centre. The majority of those in the managerial class live in the suburbs or in dormitory towns and villages up to a hundred kilometres away.

Historically, Britain has been a divided society, adversarial in the relationship between classes and institutions. The post war period of political consensus and cooperation, deriving from the shared experience of war and the ideals that created the welfare state, are now reverting to a more traditional spirit of independence and competition. The British manner of politeness, reserve and restraint which kept these in check is also giving way to thrusting individual assertiveness more in keeping with the British bulldog image.

Much rhetoric has been devoted in recent years to the breaking down of old cartels and interest groups and what is described as 'The Establishment'. This was once defined as the whole matrix of official and social relations within which power is exercised. It consists of people from a number of recognisable pillars like the Civil Service, the Conservative Party (also known as the Tory Party), the legal profession, the Church of England, Oxford and Cambridge Universities, business figures and a pool of acceptable individuals known as 'the Great and

Good'. It has proved resilient under attack, not least because it is such a fluid and almost intangible group of related interests. Some of them, such as business, have grown in importance at the expense of others, such as Oxford.

The UK is the only EC country not to have proportional representation. This favours the two main parties and a government which has a freer hand than most others in the EC. Political and legal systems are based on precedent, compromise and negotiation. There is no written constitution or bill of rights or legal code. The role of the monarch is symbolic and ceremonial rather than constitutional.

The political system epitomises the British aversion to working within a rational and systematic framework. They take pride in 'muddling through', in 'getting there in the end'. This should not necessarily be construed by outsiders as intellectual idleness. British thinking is interpretive rather than speculative. It prefers tradition and precedent and 'common sense', in other words the interpretation of experience untrammelled by theory or speculation. This usually involves finding the expedient rather than the innovative solution.

There is a deep scepticism about great schemes and constructs on a macro or a micro economic level. For example, underlying the free market ideology in fashion in the late 1980s is the belief that the economy is not susceptible to rational analysis and control and that impenetrable 'market forces' thwart attempts to channel or contain them. It also finds expression in attitudes to the European Community. There is a deep mistrust and misunderstanding of the grand design for Europe and British policy is to thwart attempts to implement it in regulatory structures. This is not regarded by the British as negativism but as pragmatism.

Business and government

There is no national agenda for economic development. The government's policy is to create a competitive environment for private business with a minimum of state intervention. Privatisation of nationalised manufacturing industries was followed by that of infrastructural and monopoly services such as water and gas. Nevertheless about one in three employees remain in public sector occupations, compared with 31 per cent in Germany and 20 per cent in Italy. There has been a major shift from manufacturing to services which now account for roughly 60 per cent of GDP and 65 per cent of the workforce. Investment in manufacturing is currently lower than it has been for a decade and decreasing.

Other than for defence contractors there is no protection against foreign takeover. Major sectors like the car industry are in foreign hands and further inward investment is actively encouraged. The UK has become the gateway for many non-EC companies into the Single Market. The UK has 120 of the 400 Japanese manufacturing facilities in Europe.

Labour

British industry is labour intensive with manual workers making up 45 per cent of the workforce, reflecting the dominance of services and the low level of capital investment. The UK is comparable with Spain and Portugal as a cheap labour market and the least restricted by labour legislation. The British prefer to work for others rather than themselves. In 1986 only 10 per cent were self-employed. About 47 per cent of employees are trade union members; 75 per cent in the public sector compared with 30 per cent of the private sector.

Union decline in industry has been matched by inroads into public sector services. Unions are organised along craft rather than industry lines which means that there may be several unions representing employees in the same company. They compete among themselves for membership and also to maintain pay differentials. Their power has been diminished by legislation, government resistance to industrial action, un-employment and falling membership in traditional manufactur-ing industry. They are no longer seen by government or employers as a partner in policy making.

Employment legislation has concentrated on curbing union power and making industrial action more difficult. Wage negotiation has been decentralised and employee protection reduced in the interest of creating a flexible labour market. Companies have a greater freedom to hire and fire than in other EC countries. Worker participation at board, or any other level, is strenuously resisted by government and business alike.

Some progress has been made, under the pressure of unemployment and low inflation, in developing negotiating practices that resort to strikes later rather than sooner, but the relationship between employers and unions remains adversarial. Pay and conditions rather than longer-term collaboration in the success of the company remain the primary union consideration.

The City

The business community is dominated by the banks, insurance companies and other financial institutions collectively known as the City. Since deregulation, large financial conglomerates have been formed. They operate within a loose legislative framework, optimistically relying on self-regulation by the institutions' own trade associations and professional bodies. Dealing institutions are regulated by the Securities and Investments Board, the SIB, whose job is to protect the interests of investors. The conduct of takeovers is supervised by the Takeover Panel, which has the power of censure but little else.

The stock market is the largest and most active in Europe and the principal source of capital for companies. There are about 4000 public limited companies (plc) with shares traded on the Stock Exchange or the Unlisted Securities Market. For smaller companies and new ventures there are various forms of private placement available. Privatisation has not significantly increased the number of active private shareholders. Institutional share-holders are far more significant in size and influence and they exert considerable influence over company managements either through informal pressure or through action in the market.

Business organisation and structure

The board of directors is the principal decision-making unit of a company and the source of power within the organisation. A plc must have a board of at least two directors appointed by the shareholders. One is the chairman who may also be the chief executive. If not, the chief executive will usually be called the managing director.

Besides the chairman there will be a company secretary, in charge of legal compliance and administration. All other board members are discretionary. There is usually a finance director and other directors representing the main operating units of the company. A holding company with a structure based on subsidiaries will have tiers of boards, usually with the same chairman. These may be called local boards consisting of local directors.

A private limited company (ltd) need only have one director appointed by the owners. Otherwise its structure and the legal framework under which it operates are very similar to the plc.

Large companies may have non-executive directors whose theoretical role is to keep an objective eye on things although their responsibilities are rarely well defined. Their real function is to provide contacts with government and the establishment. Aristocrats, politicians and retired civil servants are typical appointments. The board will then appoint an executive committee consisting of executive directors and a managing director to manage the company. This is the closest British companies get to the continental twin-board system. It is resisted by executive directors for whom it represents a curtailment of their traditional role.

Beneath board level the nature of the organisation is less clear cut. The traditionally British concept of organisation is a many layered and vertically oriented pyramid based on a vertical chain of command. Its primary purpose is seen as transmitting orders down the line from the top. In a large but declining number of companies this remains the norm. It works well in simple industries and if the people at the top know what they are doing. But for a complex organisation in a rapidly changing environment it has proved less than satisfactory.

Where top-down, structured hierarchies have been abandoned there is an antipathy towards what is pejoratively described as 'bureaucracy', procedures which have lost sight of their ultimate objective. In some cases it includes all systematic decision making procedures, clear lines of authority and channels of communication.

Organisation charts are less a map of the business than a depiction of the social hierarchy. There is a legal requirement for written job specifications but outside senior levels of management this is rarely translated into a meaningful description of specific responsibilities and goals.

In recent years there have been strenuous efforts among larger companies, assisted by a thriving training and consultancy industry, to counteract the British preference for 'muddling through' and introduce a greater degree of organisational discipline. Japanese inspired programmes with names like 'Just-In-Time' and 'Total Quality' drive concepts like meeting specifications, reliability, delivery and service through every activity in the organisation down to the way memos are typed and meetings conducted.

Planning

When asked about planning most British managers immediately think of financial forecasting and budgeting. The annual budget is the backbone of the organisation and the major exception to the otherwise inconsistent approach to systems. Most companies have a sophisticated process of annual budgeting, in some cases extended into a three or five-year forecast. Typically line managers make first drafts which are consolidated, processed, amended by senior management and fed back down to the line managers for implementation or further amendment. The forecast is monitored on a regular basis, usually monthly, and divergences explained. Bonuses and incentives may be based on meeting or outperforming forecast. The process is closely allied with the accounting function.

It is only in the largest and most sophisticated companies that this process is influenced by consideration of changes in the external environment. Planning in the sense of forecasting long-term changes in the overall environment, analysing the impact on specific markets and identifying market opportunities is rudimentary.

There is a practical reason for this in addition to the British preference for pragmatism over theory, opportunism over planning. The short-term goals of City investors do not meet the long-term needs of manufacturing investment and research. Managers are called to account primarily for quarterly earnings per share and annual dividend. In the past ten years dividend distribution in real terms has increased fourfold while invest-ment has fallen. The pressure on management is increased by the freedom given to predatory financial engineers. While they have indubitably accelerated the restructuring of British industry and improved its profitability, they encourage management to concentrate on immediate results at the expense of the longer term.

Leadership

Mr Saunders [former CEO of Guinness] had a very autocratic style. He was at the centre of a very large number of people running around outside him. He conducted the orchestra. Mr Saunders himself was the source of decisions.

Sunday Independent, 11 March 1989

Problems can only be solved by the people who have them. You have to try and coax them and love them into seeing ways in which they can help themselves.

John Harvey-Jones (former CEO of ICI)
Sunday Independent, 11 March 1989

Managers aspire to be effective, decisive and tough under the motto 'managers have a right to manage'. But these and similar macho traits, were never mentioned by any of the British I talked to when asked what qualities they looked for in their own boss. Those most often mentioned were the ability to conduct meetings efficiently and to establish good relationships with subordinates. Outsiders should be careful to distinguish between the image and the need.

It is a convention that instructions should be disguised as polite requests. People expect their boss to give them instructions and then let them get on with the job without interference. Combined with British reserve and an inbred awkwardness with personal contact it creates an arm's length relationship in which both sides are on their guard. Using the boss as a sounding board for personal or professional worries is difficult for both sides. Fairness in relationships is more important than closeness. The concept of the boss as a coach, creating an atmosphere of support and encouragement and providing constant feedback on performance, is making ground but is by no means universal.

Ambiguity and debate about the role of the boss have been exacerbated by the breakdown of hierarchical systems of control and a transition to systematic, market oriented structures. There is a wide divergence of views between companies and also within companies about the relationship between superiors and subordinates. Some attribute this to the fact that the UK is the only large EC country not to have military conscription. While the military model may not be the most appropriate in a modern business environment, and while it only concerns the male half of the workforce, it means that there is no national consensus among managers under the age of 45 about the nature of authority systems.

Teams

The British joke about their love of committees. The most important committee in a company is the board of directors. Even detailed decisions within the competence of a director may have to wait for formal approval by the board. Beneath the board is a complicated network of other committees, formal and informal.

The British prefer to work in the security of a group within an established order with which they can identify. They are motivated by work that is seen as valuable not only to themselves but others and which contributes to a common goal. The relationship between the individual and the company is expressed by the use of the word 'servant' to mean employee. It implies a strong element of duty and self-sacrifice, a personal commitment to the team in addition to the contractual arrangement.

'Individualism' in an English sense means eccentricity and non-conformism rather than self-reliance. They are uncomfortable taking individual initiatives or making a commitment unless they are confident that there is a group consensus behind them. Individuals, whatever their claims to personal responsibility, may appear vacillating and hesitant until they have cleared the matter with others.

Team members are selected for their specific expertise but their participation is expected to be general. At the same time there is a strong feeling for individual accountability for implementation. The leader's role is to embody a collective will and take personal responsibility for it while continuing to communicate and cooperate with the team. It is rare to find groups taking responsibility for error. The inclination when anything goes wrong is to find the culprit rather than looking at what can be built into the system to prevent it happening again.

Meetings

Meetings are the most important and time consuming management tool. Only the least important decisions or instructions are not formulated, discussed, approved, ratified, communicated, implemented at a meeting. They are not regarded as interruptions from real work. It is not acceptable to leave a meeting half way through, make phone calls, get on with paperwork.

Many meetings are scheduled well in advance and have comprehensive agendas. They are interspersed with others at short notice to discuss specific issues. They only start on time in companies which make a specific point of it and usually continue until all the business has been dealt with. Only the most formal end on time. The more 'creative' the participants — advertising, media and so on — the more unstructured it will be.

A meeting without a concrete result of some sort is deemed a failure. It may be a decision, the allocation of responsibilities, a series of action steps, or simply an agreement to have another meeting.

Meetings are informal in style and begin and end with social conversation. Participants are expected to make a contribution, if only questions and not necessarily in their specialist area. Opinions are encouraged and listened to but the extent to which they are taken into account depends on seniority. It is not usual for everyone to be well prepared. Even when papers are previously distributed they will not always be read. Lack of preparation does not inhibit the passing of opinion and judgement.

Passive consensus is important. A concern to avoid disharmony among the group and disloyalty to the boss will smooth over all but the most fundamental disagreement.

The process at a decision making meeting may be adversarial. A designated individual will present a proposal to the group and defend it. If it is approved he or she is mandated to implement it. It is not usual to lobby individual members beforehand, since they will not make a commitment to an idea before they have learned what the others think. Even if they have contributed to the formulation of a proposal they play an objective role at the meeting.

Communication

Formal and articulated systems for sharing information throughout the organisation are not common. Information systems are designed primarily to channel hard information to senior management and directions from them to the rest of the organisation. The technique of team briefing, in other words cascading information down through meetings of work groups, is gaining currency. It appeals both to the sense of hierarchy and the meetings culture.

Unless people are in an open office and visible to each other they will tend to use the phone in preference to a personal visit. Since the number of meetings in the working day means that people are often away from their desks, the use of internal memos is common.

Upward mobility

When asked to rank the factors influencing getting ahead in life the British put hard work, education, ambition, ability and knowing the right people (BSA Special International Report, 1989). A reputation for idleness among northern European neighbours is more attributable to inefficiency and under-investment than poor motivation.

That the British were the only nationality in the survey to put education second, rather than first, reflects a general attitude towards training and qualifications. British companies spend on average a sixth of what German and French companies spend on training. It is especially deficient at lower levels of the organisation. Four out of five manual workers and three out of five non-manual workers have received no training after leaving school. At higher levels training is regarded as a reward for promotion rather than a preparation for it.

Many science and engineering graduates are creamed off into the financial services or consultancy or accounting. This is partly because of better pay and conditions, partly because education at the highest level, even in applied subjects, is not seen as vocational. There are a small number of business schools and most universities have recently begun to offer undergraduate business-related courses. But the most valued and widespread qualification is accountancy, for which a university degree is not required. Chartered accountants proliferate not only in their field but in general management.

The prime requisite for success is performance. Nepotism and personal influence is less important. People may be selected because they are the right class or type but if they attempt to capitalise on it by 'pulling strings' they risk being rejected.

Company loyalty is less common than before the radical

corporate restructuring of the past couple of decades. It brought to management levels an experience of enforced job mobility previously confined to workers. Younger professionals incorporate a regular company move into their career planning.

Women

Women make up 45 per cent of the workforce, a larger percentage than in other countries despite having the lowest maternity benefits and negligible childcare facilities. Economic necessity and greater opportunity outweigh the difficulties. Women workers are cheaper than men and since half are part time, less protected by employment legislation.

Women are more often found in managerial positions than in most EC countries, especially in service industries and the public sector. There are fewer women in manufacturing industry although this is only partly because of discrimination. For social and educational reasons outside the workplace fewer women than men qualify in technical subjects.

Etiquette

Foreigners believe that the British are more formal than they really are. First names are used immediately among colleagues of all ranks and both sexes. It is increasingly common among all business contacts, even on the phone when there has been no personal introduction. Some men may be heard calling each other, or referring to each other, by their last names only. This is an affectation of ex-public school boys and need not be imitated. Those who have been knighted are addressed as Sir with the first name only. Doctor is only used of and to medical doctors and other academic titles are not used.

Men should not refer to themselves as Mr So-And-So. They should use the last name only or the first and last name. Women may use whichever title they prefer to be known by — Mrs, Miss or Ms and last name. There is no equivalent in a business context of the title used on its own. Superiors are sometimes called 'Sir' by male subordinates who wish to ingratiate themselves and by those in a servant role —

chauffeurs, doormen, receptionists and so on. 'Madam' is not used.

Handshaking is for first meetings and reunions. People who meet regularly do not shake hands. The greeting 'How do you do?' is not an enquiry but expects the reply 'How do you do?' and nothing more. The sensible American habit of introducing oneself, rather than waiting for an introduction to be made by the third party, is becoming widespread.

Increasing informality has not broken down the barriers of reserve. Understatement may give the impression of coolness and indifference. At the same time overt stand-offishness is avoided. Colleagues close in the hierarchy cultivate a matey, old-boy atmosphere.

The British are uneasy in situations where everyone has similar status. The complexity and subtlety of British class consciousness, with its meticulous distinctions, snobberies and snubs, is mirrored in corporate life. The principal divide is between managers and other ranks. Within these divisions there is a fine gradation marked by a host of minor privileges.

The most important symbol of rank is the car. A company car is a widespread method of tax avoidance and three quarters of new cars are bought by companies. While the company fleet is usually of the same make, the market demands a large number of superficially different models to satisfy the status requirements of its customers. The mark of superior rank is to have a car which is a different make from the company fleet and a chauffeur is a sign of absolute seniority.

On a social level it is important to be 'a nice person', meaning courteous and unassuming and unabrasive. Some older people still cultivate a gentleman amateur image. False humility and self-deprecation is more typical than self-assertion, especially by senior people with their juniors. This is changing among a younger generation who have no inhibitions about treating business seriously and energetically. 'Intellectual' is a term of disparagement. Those with a theoretical bent are advised to conceal this under a veil of pragmatism.

Politeness and reserve is reflected in conversation which is typically imprecise and vague, full of hints and subtleties, especially in the South. Facts and figures and definitive statements are avoided, as is direct confrontation and argument. For outsiders used to clarity, decisiveness and demonstrative professionalism this can be misleading. This is less true of northerners who have a reputation for plain speaking.

The British quickly lose their reserve when their basic assumptions about themselves are challenged. While they have become reconciled to losing economic and military superiority over other nations they become flustered and aggressive if moral superiority is questioned. One should not make fun of even the more outlandish traditions and customs, especially if they involve royalty. In everyday conversation it is best not to question the assumption that British television is the best in the world and British weather the most interesting.

Dress

The British are experts at classifying each other by tiny details of speech, manners and dress. Men's clothing is more an expression of affiliation than taste and the popularity of chain store off-the-peg clothing has made good tailoring optional. Ties are an important signal. Men will wear old school, army, university or club ties and, if they do not qualify, something that mimics the real thing. Since they are meant to be recognised it is not good manners to ask what they mean. It is also a social error — a 'faux pas' — to wear a tie to which you are not entitled.

Women have less of a problem. The more senior and authoritative she wishes to appear, the more her clothes should resemble men's, except that skirts not trousers should be worn.

Formal evening occasions, the annual dinner of a trade association for example, may be dignified by dinner suits which are obligatory if the invitation says 'black tie.' They need not represent a major investment since it is acceptable to hire them. At formal lunches and dinners smoking may not be permitted until after the meal. The signal for this is the 'Loyal Toast' when everyone stands up and toasts the sovereign.

Punctuality

In a social context the British have formalised unpunctuality so that it is impolite to be on time. For social occasions this means arriving between 10 and 20 minutes after the stated time. Sometimes invitations acknowledge this by specifying for example, 7.30 for 8, which means arriving no later than 7.50.

This is extended to the business sphere. People are ten minutes late for work, for meetings, for lunch. In many companies there have been recent moves to improve the efficiency and punctuality of daily life as part of the Quality movement.

Humour

There is an aversion to seriousness. Humour is expected at all levels, between all levels, and on all occasions. It is important to be entertaining on every possible occasion, public or private. There are many public figures who are not entertaining but this is regarded as a deficiency. The only public figure exempt from this expectation is the sovereign. Outsiders need not attempt to join in but should not be surprised at levity in what they might regard as inappropriate circumstances.

In a culture where the direct display of feelings is suppressed, humour is a cover for embarrassment and aggression. It can be self-deprecating, ribbing, sarcastic, sexist, jocular, racist. Women participate in humour, including sexual innuendo, with the exception of sarcasm and the needling remarks that men use to score off each other.

Socialising

Colleagues usually lunch together at work. How much mingling there is between ranks depends on circumstances. In many companies there are still segregated canteens. The directors' dining room is still common. Within a single status restaurant, although different grades may stick together, it is acceptable to take the opportunity to mingle with subordinates.

Business dinners are less common than lunches. For many a business lunch is the main meal of the day. There are no conversational rules. It depends on whether you are eating with a gentleman amateur or a dedicated professional. Actual negotiation is not usual. This takes place afterwards at the office.

Socialising at the pub immediately after work is frequent among peers and their immediate bosses. There may be some socialising among peers at weekends if they live in the same area but regular social events including partners are not common.

The preponderance of meetings and the general inefficiency of working life means that managers at all levels frequently work late hours and take work home with them. This is accepted as time for private work and only for the most urgent and informal meetings. Phone calls at home are acceptable. Working at weekends is not unknown although less common than in the USA. There is growing tendency for senior people to demonstrate indispensability by not taking full holiday entitlement.

At least once a year there will be a social occasion for all employees, often including partners. This can be as elaborate as a dinner dance in a hotel or a simple office party. Senior people are expected to make an appearance and to mingle with all employees. Intoxication and other indiscretion at the end of the evening is part of office party folklore and is not held against the miscreants thereafter.

There may also be a social club for excursions, events, a children's Christmas party. Large companies may have their own playing fields and facilities. While ranks will readily mix more senior managers are not likely to attend.

By European standards British executives are low paid so that the high life is often indulged at corporate expense. An invitation will be more for business than friendship but should nevertheless be treated as if it were a personal favour. Mostly it consists of meals but there may be invitations to socially acceptable sporting and cultural events. Partners will often be included. While often lavish and expensive, there is no taint of corruption as long as it is in a corporate context and the recipient is deemed to be a corporate representative.

BELGIUM

Belgium was created in 1830 from the Catholic provinces of the Low Countries. United in religion it remains deeply divided culturally, politically and economically into two communities identified by language. About 5.5 million of the total population of 10 million live in the northern part of the country, Flanders, and speak Flemish, a close relative of Dutch. The southern part, Wallonia, is populated by about 3.5 million French-speaking Walloons. Except for a small German speaking minority along the German border the remaining million or so live in Brussels, a predominantly French-speaking enclave in Flanders. Most Walloons cannot speak Flemish and most Flemings refuse to speak French even to foreigners. Individuals think of themselves as Walloons or Flemings first, Europeans second and Belgians third. There is a much weaker sense of national identity than in more homogeneous and nationalistic countries and a correspondingly greater enthusiasm for European federation. The monarchy and the church, both deeply conservative, are the only two national institutions of real significance.

The antipathy between the two communities goes much deeper than language. Until the 1970s Wallonia was the dominant partner, its wealth based on mining and heavy industry. Flanders was mainly agricultural, poorer and less sophisticated, except for the port city of Antwerp. The standard of living, education and public services was much higher in Wallonia. Flemish was considered the language of servants and peasants, French the language of the middle class.

The tables were turned with the collapse of the mining, steel and textile industries in Wallonia. At the same time the EC was bringing prosperity to the farmers and development to Antwerp, which competes with Rotterdam as northern Europe's entrepôt. Flanders attracted investment from its Dutch and German neighbours and other countries looking for a gateway into the rest of Europe. Its green field sites and less unionised labour force attracted new high tec industries. It is now economically the more powerful part of the country. Business people are proud of their new-found dynamism but can be resentful of continuing Walloon hegemony in the upper levels of business and the financial institutions. Middle managers feel their path to the top is blocked.

Among Walloons there is a growing realisation, especially among the young, that they are no longer automatically superior to the Flemings and even, unthinkable to an older generation, that they ought to learn Flemish if they wish to make a career inside Belgium. Some prefer to look to France for their future instead.

Meanwhile Brussels, burgeoning home to Eurocrats, Nato-crats and regional headquarters of multinational corporations, has been able to remain neutral. As its role as a national capital becomes less commanding, the city is making a concerted effort to become the capital of Europe. Geographically part of Flanders, it is 75 per cent French speaking and English is increasingly acceptable in international business as well as public places. About a quarter of its residents are non- Belgian. While the city as a whole becomes increasingly cosmopolitain the Flemish minority is increasingly fearful of being swamped and their sensitivities should be recognised in everyday dealings.

In 1989 political disintegration culminated in the creation of two virtually autonomous regions and a number of 'Communi-ties', including Brussels. Domestic functions have been handed over but many of the national institutions remain intact. For example most ministries are duplicated on a national and regional level — there are now about 65 ministers in all — and their responsibilities are not clearly defined. Meanwhile the three main political parties, Socialist, Democrat and Liberal, have divided along linguistic lines with varying degrees of acrimony — the two halves of the Socialist Party fight but the Liberals work together. The transition to what many Belgians believe will be a fully fledged federal state is clearly not yet over.

Business environment

Belgium is heavily dependent on international trade. Like the Netherlands, about 60 per cent of GNP is accounted for by exports. Antwerp, the third largest port in the world, is the rival to Rotterdam as a gateway to the rest of Europe. It is also a target for foreign, mainly French investment. The central pillar of the business establishment, the *Société Générale de Belgique* was recently taken over by the French Suez group after a debilitating battle with the Italian financier Carlo de Benedetti. *La Générale* is a holding company reputed to control a third of Belgium's industry. It owns the largest bank and major companies such as Fina and Solvay.

Direct state participation in industry is small and relatively recent. State owned holding companies (SNI, SRIW, SRIB, GOMV) either ease the restructuring of lame-duck industries or provide venture capital for private investment in high tec industries. There are direct investment incentives for private companies designed to reduce unemployment and foster high tec projects and tax breaks for foreign multinationals setting up regional headquarters.

Three labour organisations correspond with the main political parties. They negotiate on a regional level with the employers' organisation, VBO–FEB (*Verbond der Belgische Ondernemingen–Fédération des Entreprises Belges*) or on an industry basis. The relationship is generally regarded as reasonable and cooperative and characterised by compromise rather than confrontation.

All companies of more than 100 employees are obliged to set up a works council with equal numbers of management and employee representatives. Every company with more than 50 employees must set up a safety committee as well.

It is usually obvious whether a company is Walloon or Flemish from the initials after its name. Flemish companies are either NV if public or BVBA if private (*Naamloze Vennootschapp* or *Beslote Vennootschapp met Beperkte Aansprakelijkheid*). Walloon companies are SA or SPRL (*Société Anonyme* or *Société Privée à Responsabilité Limitée*). The shareholders of an SA-NV elect a minimum of three directors and a statutory auditor. The owners of a SPRL-BVBA appoint one or more directors. It is unusual for the board of directors to include more than the managing director from among the managers of the company.

Organisation and leadership

Walloons and Flemings have less in common with their French and Dutch neighbours than many outsiders assume. They also have more in common with each other than either would like to admit. There is a recognisably Belgian approach to many social and business issues.

The Belgian solution is based on compromise. Adaptability, flexibility, intellectual humility and an avoidance of dogmatism sets Belgians apart from their immediate neighbours. A preference for the middle way came out in all my conversations with foreigners and Belgians alike. It is hard to pin down a definitive style, an elusiveness which some outsiders characterise as blandness. There is a greater concern to find a solution than· to win the argument. The process is gradualist, pragmatic and to more effervescent outsiders agonisingly deliberate. Despite this, the end result can be surprising and creative. A classic example from the political sphere occurred in April 1990 when the King felt that his conscience would not allow him to give his assent to abortion legislation passed by parliament. So he abdicated for a day.

Compromise is combined with conservatism. There is a reluctance to embrace novelty if the old ways still work. This includes views about the role of women which are among the most traditional in Europe. There are very few women professional managers and the exceptions are primarily in family owned companies.

Flanders

In dealing with Flemings in any circumstance it is vital to acknowledge their sensitivity about speaking French, whether or not it is your first language. Even if French is the language that you have most easily in common, it is advisable to struggle through a few words of Dutch or English or German, after which you will be invited to use French.

Although Flemings often refer to their language as Dutch it is more mannered and ornate than the version spoken by their more plain spoken neighbours. There is a similar distinction in tastes and manners. Flemings enjoy good food and living well and other un-Calvinist indulgences. They are also more outwardly formal. Progressing from *Mejneer* and *Mevrouw* with the last name to first name terms takes longer than with the Dutch, if it happens at all, and the polite plural is more common than the informal singular. Nevertheless, relationships are relaxed and low-key. Assertiveness in manner and speech is likely to be interpreted as arrogance.

Unless the targets are Walloons or Dutch, humour tends to be mild and self-deprecating rather than ebullient, good humoured rather than funny. In a business context it is acceptable in informal circumstances but to make jokes and banter at the beginning of a meeting or during a presentation is regarded by all Belgians as an Anglo-Saxon eccentricity.

Organisational structures are flat and procedures unsophisticated. Offices tend to be simple and functional. Titles, type of office, perks and other status symbols are far less important than take-home pay. There are few company cars so what you drive is to impress the neighbours rather than establish rank among colleagues.

The Flemish approach is characterised more by conscientiousness than imagination. French managers may be better at designing systems — and then ignoring them — while Flemings more disciplined in applying them. In more traditional companies hierarchical lines and formal channels of communication are adhered to but tempered with active and informal networking, ad hoc meetings and so on.

Flemings prefer participative authority and leadership. The boss is expected to be approachable, to 'walk the job' and to base his or her authority on competence rather than hierarchical position. They expect participative decision making, active consensus and delegation of responsibility.

Wallonia

Walloons resent being regarded as quaint Frenchmen. Like the Irish in Britain their achievements tend to be subsumed into their more powerful neighbour while their eccentricities, like their accent, are made fun of. There is a risk in describing their attitudes to organisation as a watered down version of the French.

While they regard themselves as more punctual, harder working and more practical than the French, there are similarities in a preference for a structured, formal organisation with a clear hierarchical system and for a directive style of leadership. Rules and procedures are important and in the main adhered to. Distinctions of rank are important with attention paid to job title, size of office, quality of furniture, parking space and so on. While subordinates will feel free to contribute information and suggestions to the boss it is a clear expectation that the decision is his or hers alone. Once taken and promulgated in writing it will not be questioned. Whether it will be carried out may depend on the boss's competence in following up. Traditional relationships between managers and subordinates are distant and formal although a younger generation of managers is slowly introducing a more egalitarian style.

Meetings are more for exchanging information and discussing alternative proposals than for decision making which is not regarded as the function of a group. Indeed little importance is given to groups in any context and working relationships are primarily vertically oriented.

All this is subject to the Belgian talent for compromise and negotiation. Because Belgians avoid extremes and season everything they do with common sense there is less perceptible difference between what is supposed to happen and what actually does. For other Northern Europeans this more transparent and less dogmatically assertive environment is more comfortable. The most noticeable difference with France is in problem solving and decision making. While French take an inductive, dogmatic approach Belgians are deductive and pragmatic.

Etiquette is more traditional than in France. The transition from *Monsieur* or *Madame* with last names and the polite plural to first names and the informal singular takes longer, and is for close colleagues in informal circumstances. Sense of humour has a Gallic preference for wit and irony, usually at someone else's expense. The main difference is that Belgians can laugh at themselves. Just as Irish have the best Irish jokes and Jews the best Jewish jokes, Belgians have the best Belgian jokes.

DENMARK

Among member countries the Danes share with the British the least enthusiasm for the EC. In public opinion surveys carried out by Eurobarometer in the spring of 1989, 25 per cent of the sample said they would be relieved if it were scrapped. Their opinion is not uninformed. They also have the highest percentage of those who declare they are interested in EC politics.

With a population of 5 million they feel swamped by the other 300 million or so. Their highly developed but small and specialised economy is perceived as having little to gain either from a mass market or from the financial and other benefits that some other countries expect from Brussels. Many would feel more comfortable with their fellow Scandinavians outside the Community.

Business environment

The Danish temperament is unsuited to corporatism, whether on a national or international scale. The image of Denmark as a model welfare state based on coalition and conformity, while accurate, should not obscure a deep commitment to autonomy and independence. The workforce of about 400,000 is spread among 6000 companies — more than half is employed by firms with fewer than 200 employees. Agriculture is based on small farms and smallholdings in a network of cooperatives and the fishing industry is made up of owner-captains rather than commercially run fleets.

All Danish industry and agriculture is in private hands. An entrepreneurial outlook combined with the small size of the industrial base has led to a strategy based on the exploitation of specialist market niches.

Organisation

Public Limited Companies have a supervisory board, *Bestyrelse*, elected by the shareholders. They appoint the management board, *Direktion*. Sometimes members of the management board can be elected to the Supervisory Board as long as they are in a minority. In companies employing more than 35 people the employees are entitled to elect to the Supervisory Board, half the number of members elected by the shareholders. In companies with more than 30 employees they or the employer can opt for a works council to be set up, *samarbejdsudvalg*, consisting of equal numbers of management and employee representatives.

There are many similarities with the business culture of their North Sea neighbours, the Dutch. Organisations are transparent and the hierarchy purely functional. There is a lot of sideways communication between areas and there is a readiness to cut across the hierarchy if necessary.

The boss is considered a coach or team leader to the group. Authority is based on professionalism and competence and an authoritarian manner is considered rude and unnecessary. Especially among the younger generation there is an emphasis on open communication and consultation at all levels and to share objectives and goals. If something goes wrong the priority is to bring it out into the open and take steps to make sure it does not happen again.

While accountability lies with individuals they will rarely take decisions before consultation with everyone affected. Meetings are frequent. They can be briefing, discussion or decision making but it is always made clear what sort it is. They have always a stated purpose, an agenda, and they will start and end punctually. It is more important to keep to the timetable than come to a conclusion. If something is not covered properly the participants will reconvene. Preparation for meetings and indeed any discussion is very important. At the same time, lobbying before a meeting may be considered underhand — everybody might not get the same picture.

All participants are encouraged to voice a considered opinion but consensus is less important than being fully informed. If a vote is taken or the boss makes the decision everyone will go along with it.

Upward mobility

There is a greater sense of corporate pride than in many countries and it is rare to job hop. Promotion is on the basis of performance and professionalism.

Among EC countries Denmark has the highest proportion of women in the workforce. There are comprehensive maternity benefits, paternity leave and child care provision. Women are commonly found in managerial and professional jobs and there is little discrimination against them.

Etiquette and behaviour

Among older people and new acquaintances the polite *Die* and the last name is customary. Among younger people the informal *Du* and first names are common.

Like the Dutch, Danes are plain speaking. Frankness is a sign of honesty and reliability, as is meticulous punctuality in business and social life.

Social values are egalitarian. Despite a high standard of living, ostentation is frowned upon and the outward trappings of success meet with disapproval.

Humour

People try to be good humoured rather than humorous. Humour is not out of place in a business context but it is rarely sarcastic or self-deprecating or flippant. Irony may be misunderstood by the literal minded.

Social life

There is often a canteen. If not, people bring sandwiches. Lunch breaks are short and it is rare to go out. Lunch is not part of the business day and there is little business entertaining. There is mingling of ranks but this does not serve a business purpose. People want to turn off for half an hour.

Everyone goes home at five in the evening and there is little social mixing between colleagues outside work. What there is usually takes place at home over an early dinner. Entertaining is informal, except for the Scandinavian custom of synchronised drinking and choruses of *sköl*. The typical atmosphere is a cosy conviviality described by the word *hygge*, whose best translation is probably 'snug.'

GREECE

Despite a tradition of political and economic crisis it would not be accurate to say that confidence in government has been damaged. It was never very high to begin with. The government's primary role is seen as redistributing money and whether you are on the giving or receiving end depends on your ingenuity.

Outsiders should be careful not to confuse what they regard as civic irresponsibility with lack of patriotism. This is embodied in religion and language and a strong sense of history. Although they are happy to play along with the romantic notion that they are descendants of the Ancient Greeks, their true antecedent is Byzantium, which they have kept alive in institutions and customs throughout centuries of foreign domination. Constantinople not Athens is the real spiritual home.

While Greeks are rightfully resentful of what they perceive as outside interference, they are anything but chauvinistic. Aptitude and necessity have given them an international outlook. The worldwide shipping industry, trading communities in every continent, and prosperous emigrant communities, bear witness to an immensely enterprising and adaptable people.

Greek life as well as language is demotic. Social hierarchies sit uneasily on Greek society. The basic social unit is the family closely followed by the *xorio*, or village. This is not a geographical or community concept but a close network of family alliances. This survives even in the context of the Athens conurbation, where almost half the Greek population lives.

Business environment

The traditional backbone of Greek industry had been large conglomerates run by dynastic families and closely associated with the banks, notably the National Bank of Greece. With the coming of the socialist PASOK party to power, 30 of the largest conglomerates were nationalised and their managements replaced with political appointees of varying levels of competence. The state now controls some 70 per cent of economic activity either directly or through the banks.

Second in importance is the multitude of small family owned companies. Nimble and entrepreneurial these companies have learned to be opportunistic and flexible, if they have survived a record number of bankruptcies in the past two years. Some have been replaced by new businesses set up by entrepreneurs returning from abroad.

Foreign investment has been targetted on tourist-related industries, such as hotels and food and beverage companies. This remains the most buoyant sector with eight million visitors a year.

Industrial relations are politicised, confrontational and unstructured. The ministry of labour actively controls the pay structure by fiat. In order to compensate staff for performance and discourage them from leaving, companies have to resort to perks, bonuses and subterfuge. They are also used to induce people not to take two jobs. This common practice is partly to earn money and partly to build up the personal business to which most Greeks aspire.

Organisation

Corporate structure is based either on the French SA model, Anonymi Eteria, (AE) or the Limited Company, Eteria Periorismenis Efthinis, (EPE). An AE has a board of at least three directors elected by shareholders. The chief executive is either the General Manager *Genikos Dieftindis* or the managing director *Diefthinon Simvoulos*. The former is usually associated with the SA and the latter with an EPE although sometimes the two positions can be found in the same company.

In a traditional company the titles and positions are irrelevant. There is one boss, the *effendikos*, who takes all responsibility. He is the owner or has the owner's trust. Below him is a narrow and vertically oriented hierarchy of subordinates who are delegated specific tasks and little responsibility.

This approach works better in small and medium sized family companies than in large or state owned companies. Unless they have trained or worked in a large company abroad Greeks are uncomfortable in such an environment. Greek and Italian mentality should not be confused but their attitude to corporate life is very similar. Organisations exist solely for the benefit of the individuals within it.

Banks are instrumental in introducing management discipline. The cash flow forecast is the most important piece of financial information, coupled with a one year or eighteen month operating plan. They expect to see a proper management structure and a realistic organisation chart. Some multi-nationals and a few of the state owned companies have introduced other American-inspired practices. There are a growing number of young people educated in business schools in the UK and the USA, returning emigrants from Australia, America and Europe, who bring back with them new attitudes and practices.

While procedural mechanisms may be drawn up they are not always adhered to, especially if they run laterally rather than vertically across the organisation. The quality of cooperation between departments depends largely on the personal relationships of those concerned.

Forecasts and plans are the preserve of senior management and remain subject to constant amendment. The plan is a tool for negotiating with banks and shareholders rather than a management device. Time horizons are short and there is a preference for opportunistic, reactive policies.

Leadership

Traditional leadership styles are highly directive in that individual rather than group responsibility is paramount. But they sit uneasily on a preference for collective action. *Parea*, or company, is an essential feature of Greek life. This by no means implies unanimity. To be a member of any group, formal or informal, carries with it the obligation to make a distinctive contribution. This combination of extreme individualism and collectivism can be confusing to outsiders. It can be very productive in a small and paternalistic environment but frequently leads to factionalism in larger organisations.

Meetings

The meeting is a forum for the dynamic expression of strong personal opinions, preferably contrary to everyone else's. Everyone may have their turn and will be listened to and energetically argued with.

Formal meetings are arranged only for important issues. Frequent informal coordination and briefing meetings are a valuable method of finding out what is going on when information systems are crude and unreliable. There is seldom a formal agenda and rarely are there formal minutes, other than the ones individual participants take. Consensus is important. As long as there is not compromise or unanimity the meeting will be reconvened.

Communication

Personal contact is important in the smallest matters. Only when it is impossible to meet face-to-face will the telephone be used, and then at great length. Information and gossip is hoarded and swapped on a transactional basis.

There is a distrust of written communication. The recipient of a letter or memo will ask not what it says but why does the sender want a permanent record. Also, written Greek is difficult, even for Greeks. Until relatively recently there was a separate written language, *katherevousa*. Letters and memos still tend to be stilted and formal and there is a lot of snobbery about how well you write. Orally however, there are no constraints. In today's populist environment simple, demotic Greek is preferred and regional accents are acceptable.

Upward mobility

The major consideration for preferment is whether the person concerned can be trusted rather than qualifications, expertise or performance. This is the basis of the nepotism, political affiliation and personal influence, known in Greek as *messon*, which permeate the fabric of every Greek organisation. The technocratic ideal of rising to the top on merit and performance alone is honoured in the breach in all European cultures but rarely more than in Greece.

Trust is the basis on which outsiders are judged as well. They are genuinely welcomed as a source of new ideas and expertise, international contacts and influence but any suspicion that they are exploiting the relationship or attempting to dominate it will be detrimental. It is unwise to join in the politics even if there appear to be factions or individuals who want you on their side. Greeks are world champions at such things and in the end the loyalty of Greek to Greek is stronger.

Compared with most European countries there is little discrimination against women. They are well represented in the professions and politics and their opportunities in business, like those of the men, depend more on their connections than their sex.

Etiquette and behaviour

The language is extraordinarily rich and difficult and further complicated by the alphabet. Knowing other languages or Ancient Greek is not much help. Greeks are well aware of this and even a smattering reaps richer rewards than in other countries and will be treated with infinite patience.

There is a subtle range of formality in the way Greeks

address each other but this need not be inhibiting to an outsider. Any attempt to address them in Greek will be regarded as a compliment. *Kyrie* or *Kyria* can be used with the first or last name and the polite plural or informal singular can be used with either. Kyrie or Kyria can be used on their own. First names are used between colleagues of similar age and status and sometimes last names. The formality of first acquaintance will rapidly move to informality. If in doubt ask, but you will probably have been told first.

Outside the banks dress is more informal than in most other European countries. It is also a poor guide to status. The only consistency is that it is not usual to dress up to go to work or dress down to enjoy oneself.

Humour

Humour is as frequently enjoyed in business as anywhere else. It is witty, satirical and pointed, especially where government is concerned. Among people with a close relationship it can be uninhibited and personal. This applies not only to humour. Pretentiousness and stand-offishness is not appreciated. Comparative strangers may quizz you about family circumstances and personal finances.

Greeks are skilled debaters and employ a whole gamut of verbal and physical expressions. To outsiders used to a more restrained mode of expression what appears like a full blown argument may be a quite innocuous exchange of views. The time to beware is when your interlocutor becomes quiet and withdrawn.

Socialising

The official working day starts early and ends at lunchtime when most people go home although large companies are increasingly changing to northern European hours. Breaks for coffee and snacks are a seamless part of the day. Lunchtime entertaining is usually for business guests.

More formal occasions at the office, such as the ceremonial cutting of the New Year cake, are attended by most people but are not occasions of social mixing. Larger companies may organise social events for those lower down in the organisation. Out of hours mixing among colleagues results from social compatibility and not business reasons and there is little mingling among ranks.

IRELAND

Eire is only used in Gaelic. In English it should be referred to as Ireland.

Gaelic is an official language in Ireland and Brussels. While fewer than 100,000 people, living mostly in the rural areas of the west of Ireland, speak it as a first language, it has sentimental and nationalist importance. It is taught in schools and government servants, including teachers, must pass an examination in it as a condition of employment. It is not used in business.

Ireland is the newest of the EC countries. In 1922 the island was partitioned between the six counties of Ulster, which remained part of the United Kingdom, and the other 26, which formed the Irish Free State, a Dominion in the British Commonwealth. It became a fully independent Republic in 1949.

It is a small island economy with a predominantly rural tradition. The population is 3.5 million of whom a million live in Dublin, the only major city. The main regional difference is between the dispersed rural areas and the urban middle classes of Dublin. Hopes and aspirations for an egalitarian society after the departure of the British have been unfulfilled. One of their several legacies is an elaborate class system based on education, wealth, and professional status.

United Ireland

The predominant unifying force is the Roman Catholic church to which over 90 per cent of the population belongs. The cultural influence of its conservative brand of Catholicism, in all forms of social and political life, differentiates Ireland from Britain and fosters attitudes and beliefs which are more akin to southern than northern Europe. For example, the concept of power being invested in a centralised and directive authority, rather than shared between essentially independent individuals and groups, is Latin rather than Anglo-Saxon and is reflected in a preference for autocratic rather than participative leadership.

The major political parties are unique in Europe in that they do not represent defined social or economic interest groups. Fianna Fail is descended from those who voted against partition in 1922 in the interests of a united Ireland, and Fine Gael from those who voted for immediate independence.

Partition and its consequences distort the image that Ireland presents to the world. The Northern Ireland question is a political responsibility and unification is an ultimate ideal which few would consider feasible in their lifetime — or desirable. The impact of a million Protestants and the IRA would be considered disruptive and unpredictable. It is not a domestic political issue. Sinn Fein, the political wing of the IRA, has marginal political support and the events over the border are for most Irish citizens as remote as for British subjects over the water.

Economy

An unprecedented boom in the economy through the late 1960s and 1970s led to the development of a welfare state that can no longer be afforded. Corporate taxes of 50 per cent, the highest personal taxes and VAT rates in the EC stifle the economy and have led to recent severe cutbacks in public spending.

The economy is inextricably linked with Britain's through geographic proximity and centuries of colonial dependence. With little industrial heritage or natural resources its role was to provide foodstuffs to Britain in return for manufactured goods. The UK still accounts for 35 per cent of Irish exports and 42 per cent of imports.

Ireland's most consistent export is enterprising and energetic people. Apart from the period of economic expansion in the sixties and seventies emigration has characterised Irish demographics. Between 1987 and 1989 about 100,000, mainly young people, have left. This is the equivalent of about 8 per cent of a workforce of 1.3 million — a considerable number. Britain, where the Irish have full rights of citizenship, and the United States have the largest and most influential Irish communities.

While emigration reduces the social and economic pressures of unemployment the price is the breakdown of families and communities and perpetuates economic mismanagement and complacency.

Foreign investment

The economy has traditionally been state led with direct government ownership, employment schemes, subsidies and tax breaks. Ten per cent of the non-agricultural work-force is in the state sector. Apart from utilities and monopoly services the state has direct investments in insurance, air, land and sea transportation, hotels, fertilisers, sugar, steel and horse racing. The private sector is marked by a concentration of power in the hands of a few individuals and companies primarily involved in agriculture and food.

After an isolationist period immediately following independence Ireland adopted a policy of open trade and the encouragement of foreign investment. Initially this was extremely successful and involved companies in clean and advanced technology industries like electronics and pharmaceuticals. Foreign penetration of business is the highest in Europe. There are now over 900 majority foreign owned companies controlling 50 per cent of total turnover and employing 40 per cent of the non-agricultural work force. The largest number of companies, 344, are American and the second largest, 235, are British. Germans come third with 136.

The policy has been less successful in creating an environment for self-sustaining industrial growth. Part of the reason is the small size of the home market, obliging successful Irish companies to expand abroad. Six of the largest Irish companies have overseas investments accounting for over 80 per cent of annual turnover.

Organisation

Company structure is similar to Britain's. There is no significant difference between the structures of public and private limited companies. The board can elect one of its members as Managing Director or appoint a General Manager. Supervisory boards are not recognised in law or practice and employees have no representation rights on the board. Many companies have works councils with rights of negotiation with, and representation to, management.

The Irish arguably have a more flexible approach to organisation than the British. This is reflected in the importance given to personal relationships, a talent for improvisation and a dislike of rigid systems and bureaucracy. However the old image of quaint inefficiency is a thing of the past, if it was ever true. The workforce is by overall European standards young, well educated, computer literate and professional.

In common with their British neighbours the Irish have a highly pragmatic and unintellectual approach to problems. They are more traders and dealers than long-term investors and short-termism characterises their approach to planning and strategy.

Among the younger generation the traditional antipathy towards women in business is losing ground although general attitudes towards women in the workplace remain traditional and conservative. The Irish and the Belgians share the greatest antipathy in the EC towards working women.

There is an outward deference to authority combined with strong reservations about accepting it. The role of the boss and the way in which he or she is regarded by subordinates is more Gallic than Anglo-Saxon. The boss expects to have to impose his or her will.

Etiquette

Etiquette and modes of address are similar to those in the UK but Irish manners are less reserved and considerably more amiable, relaxed and gregarious. There is a pervasive informality and an antipathy towards pretence and pretension. This can be misleading. In the practicalities of negotiation they are anything but easy-going. Amiable frankness is combined with astuteness and often stubbornness.

Among those I talked to, the Irish were the only ones to complain about a British lack of a sense of humour at work. Great store is set by 'crack', whose meaning should not be confused with American English. It means fun in the sense of good humour and can range from crude anecdotes to subtle wit before which nothing, even the sacred, is sacred.

LUXEMBOURG

The most significant feature of this chapter is that it exists at all. Luxembourgers celebrated with pointed enthusiasm the 150th anniversary of their independence in 1989 and they find every opportunity to remind visitors of it — albeit, being Luxembourgers, in a most polite and unassuming way.

Luxembourg is usually lumped in with Belgium with which it joined in a monetary and tariff union in 1922. In 1944 the Netherlands joined them to form Benelux, the prototype of the EC. While Benelux provides a political and economic orientation Luxembourg's primary business orientation is towards Germany. In most companies the lingua franca is German, both spoken and written.

Their sense of identity is based on language, Luxembourgisch. It is spoken mainly at home and on social occasions. It causes great resentment that foreigners who have lived and worked there for many years do not take the trouble to learn even a few words. Not that there is much incentive. Luxembourgers of all levels learn and speak French and German as fluently as their own language. Nearly half the population speaks at least two foreign languages and 40 per cent three or more.

Business environment

There are not many Luxembourg companies and the chances of readers working with one are statistically small. If they do work in Luxembourg they are more likely to be employed by one of the hundred or so international banks or the multinationals which use it as a European distribution centre. In many ways Luxembourg provides an interesting example of what results when the different business cultures of northern Europe meet.

The population of Luxembourg is about 400,000 and the workforce is about 160,000. Despite the rationalisation of the steel industry, Luxembourg's traditional indigenous industry, there is little unemployment. A third of the workforce comprises frontier commuters from Belgium, France and Germany and longer-term immigrant workers, mainly from the EC. Luxembourg has learned to manage this cosmopolitan workforce, drawn from all over Europe, without a major strike since 1922. Folklore has it that since the last war there was one strike lasting one day starting on Friday afternoon. Absenteeism is low — government sources put it at less than five per cent.

Unemployment can be controlled and troublemakers weeded out with the closely monitored work permit system. Nevertheless Luxembourg embodies in miniature a collaborative and institutionalised approach to industrial relations. While employers find it irksome and employees often have to be urged by their representatives to take an interest, it is associated with productivity rates which are much higher than those of countries which have a confrontational approach. The basis is a complex legal and administrative framework for negotiation and conciliation at factory and national level.

Business structure

Every company over 15 employees must have an elected staff representative committee. If there are over a 100 employees there are several committees representing white collar, manual and, if there are enough, an under 21's committee. In companies employing more than 1000 a third of the board of directors is elected by the staff committee. All employees in the country elect their representatives at the same time every four years.

In addition, any company employing more than 150 has to have a Joint Works Council consisting of an equal number of management representatives, appointed by the chief executive, and employees, elected in a secret ballot with proportional representation. The Council must be consulted on financial results, investment plans, changes in production methods and so on in addition to terms and conditions of employment.

Organisation

For many years the Luxembourg economy was based on the steel industry. Around it were gathered numerous family owned businesses, mainly in steel fabrication and tools, united in a cosy relationship with each other, the banks the government and the unions. The traditional Luxembourg business culture, still in evidence in older established companies, follows a French/Belgian pattern of a strict hierarchy under an autocratic *patron*. Major decision making is a private affair between family members. Formal meetings are for briefing and formalising decisions made by the boss with input from relevant experts.

More recently founded and entrepreneurial companies, managed by young cadres educated abroad, are developing a new style of management based on participation and informality of decision making and communication.

There is no university in Luxembourg. So professionals, whether, Luxembourger or foreign, are recruited from universities and business schools all over Europe. This results in a mix of backgrounds and cultures which can be very productive but can also lead to interesting comparison of . national character. One chief executive who deliberately recruits a mix of nationalities described French and Italians expert at projecting and selling themselves, Germans as clinically honest and accurate about their strengths and weaknesses, Luxembourgers as overmodest.

Etiquette

Luxembourgers tend to be reserved both in business and private life, which they keep clearly separate. The working atmosphere will generally be collaborative and consensus orientated, so it is not wise to assert a position unless you are very sure of your ground — and even then in a modest way. Assertiveness, strong criticism and especially personal remarks, even if meant lightheartedly or humorously, are seen as aggressive and rude. Outside working hours, outsiders often have to take the initiative to establish social relationships — a few words of Luxembourgisch go a long way.

If the modest and bourgeois social values of Luxembourg seem claustrophobic to more extrovert outsiders it is perhaps part of the price a small community has to pay for autonomy, social harmony and one of the highest and most equitable standards of living in Europe.

PORTUGAL

The Portuguese are an Atlantic not a Mediterranean nation. It is an error as well as a social gaffe to lump Portugal and Spain together. Until the 1974 revolution orientation was towards Africa, where it had a colonial relationship with Angola, and South America, where trading links with Brazil are still strong. The exception was a strong connection with the UK, through the port wine trade. One thing they have in common with Spain is a marked about-face towards Europe following political change and membership of the EC.

The 1974 Revolution was followed by nationalisation of banking and industry consisting primarily of textiles, chemicals, ship-building and repair. The state directly owns about 70 companies and another 80 indirectly, accounting for about 50 per cent of the country's industrial assets. This is now being dismantled by a privatisation programme begun in 1989. The state still maintains 51 per cent although recent legislation may by now have made it possible for 100 per cent private ownership. Throughout this period the private sector continued to be dominated by a dozen families which have begun to reassert themselves, although a handful of new entrepreneurs are beginning to challenge their hegemony.

Organisation

The traditional corporate structure of a public corporation, *Sociedade Anonima de Responsibilidade Limitada*, (SA), con-

140

tains a Board of Directors, *Conselho de Administraçao*, and a Board of Auditors, *Conselho Fiscal*, which is composed of shareholder representatives. More modern companies have a Management Board, *Direcçao*, made up of no more than five directors appointed by the General Board, *Conselho General*. The latter is elected by a shareholders' meeting. They also appoint a shareholder as Statutory Auditor *Revisor Oficial de Contas* whose responsibilities should not be confused with an independent auditor.

A *Sociedade por Quotas de Responsibilidade Limitada*, (Lda) is managed by a director appointed by the owners. There are no other boards or officers.

There are workers committees empowered to inspect and comment on financial information and terms and conditions of employment.

While the revolution changed many aspects of Portuguese social and political life it left the civil service and its methods virtually intact. The large state owned companies are compartmentalised and bureaucratic. Smaller companies and private companies have the more unstructured style of a family company. Organisations are based on a vertical personal hierarchy rather than a systematic division of responsibility under strong control from the top.

Leadership is essentially directive with a concentration of power at the top of the organisation working through a chain of command based on personal loyalty rather than systematic delegation. Delegation is to the person one trusts rather than the position they hold. Subordinates are given little power or responsibility. This extends to the secretary's control of the diary.

Organisational procedures tend to be vague and negotiable and there is what outsiders may regard as a cavalier attitude towards delivery dates and similar commitments. Management information systems and financial budgeting tend to be rudimentary. Sales volume and cash flow are the key indicators.

Meetings

Meetings are for briefing and discussion and are not expected to be implemental. They are not considered an appropriate forum for decision making or delegation or to have a clear, decisive result.

Meetings, like most appointments, are unlikely to start on time. There will be an agenda but people will not feel bound by it and individuals may leave for other pressing business. The formality of making contributions through the chair is not generally widespread.

Unless a senior person is present, who will automatically dominate proceedings, everyone feels free to make a contribution. The aim is not to find common ground but to express a point of view as emphatically as possible and preferably in contradiction with everyone else's. Flexible and collaborative in private, the public forum is for competitive self-assertion. If agreement or support for a proposal is required at a meeting it is essential to have lobbied the participants in private beforehand. Otherwise they are likely to disagree on principle.

Upward mobility

The traditional business élite was based on old family-owned commercial groups. They have been joined by their entre-preneurial managers who left to set up their own companies. There is a growing professional managerial class many of whom are educated abroad or at the business school at the Catholic University.

Etiquette

As well as the titles *Senhor* and *Senhora* Portuguese make indiscriminate use of *Doutor* with anyone suspected of having a University degree. They also use the titles *Engenheiro* and *Arquitecto* when appropriate. There is a familiar and polite form of address, *tu* and *você*. *Tu* is only used with people who have more than a business relationship and are equal or close in status. There are several possible combinations of tu and você with first and last names and titles, deriving from a refined sense of hierarchy. The deferential *O Senor* and *O Senhora*, without a name, is then used. The most important thing to remember is to avoid tu with subordinates and junior people unless you have known them a long time.

Spanish speakers will be understood although they should be prepared for one-sided conversations as replies in Portuguese will be very difficult to understand. It is a language rich in phonics as well as literature. There are 13 vowel sounds associated with the letter 'a' alone.

Portuguese is the self-styled country of *brandos costumes* — soft customs. They are quiet and understated. Business relationships are essentially personal and informal. While they prefer to avoid confrontation they are individually competitive and wary of losing out to their peers.

Dress is based around the jacket and tie and varies in formality with the seasons. There is little distinction between dressing for work and for social life.

Normal working hours are eight to five with two hours for lunch but are flexible. The business day includes long lunches and relaxed dinners at restaurants. The habit of going home for lunch is waning and colleagues will eat together at restaurants. Otherwise they do not get together socially.

Business and private life are intermingled. Evening meetings and telephone calls at home are common and often necessary to compensate for missed appointments during the day.

AMERICANS IN EUROPE

American management theory and practice pervade European business. This is partly a consequence of the high level of direct investment. In many countries and industries Americans are the leading foreign investors and may even dominate domestic interests. Their influence is compounded by international consulting and accountancy industries, imbued with American ideas and methods.

Indirect influence is also pervasive. Much European business education is modelled on American theories and teaching methods. For example, many of the core theories of people management taught at European business schools are based on original research carried out in the USA in the first half of the century. The resources available to American business academia are much greater, and its status much higher, than in many countries in Europe. In the more popular domain, the gurus who sell most books and claim biggest audiences are American.

The motivation for looking at the American example is that, at least until Japan provided an alternative, the American way was the most successful. And with success goes chic. Just as Europe adopted English dress, manners and jargon at the end of the nineteenth century, so it has adopted Americana in the twentieth. In every European country those managers who seek to an alternative for their traditional style look to the USA. It is also neutral. It is more comfortable for most Europeans to follow the American model than, say, the German, which has had comparable success.

American business culture is much more varied than European preconceptions allow. Our direct experience is mainly limited to multinationals and their expatriate employees, not necessarily typical of either the parochial or the enterpreneurial sectors of their domestic environment. The following remarks are limited to those aspects which create the greatest misunderstanding between Europeans and expatriate Americans.

Organisation

The influential theories associated with the term 'Scientific Management' originated in the USA and are based on the belief that organisational processes can be systematically analysed and improved. All the processes of the organisation down to minor reports and decisions are subject to detailed quantitative analysis. Planning, both in the sense of budgeting and also wider strategic planning, is detailed and taken seriously. Areas of management which in Europe would be left to qualitative assessment, for example human resource management, are subject to systematic analysis. To Europeans this can seem unnecessary or impractical but Americans view unsubstantiated and unquantified assertions with scepticism.

As the environment changes so the organisational functions necessary to cope with it are very quickly changed too. The immediate reaction to a development in the business or technological environment, or to a change of management, is to change the organisation. A characteristic of American corporate life is constant upheaval in which social hierarchies and relationships are repeatedly disturbed.

Organisations exist independently of their members. The needs of individuals are seen as subsidiary to the needs of the organisation. Each member has a well-defined function to carry out and if that particular function no longer has any part to play, then neither does the person doing it. The readiness of companies to fire surplus or underperforming employees and the corresponding readiness of employees to change companies in order to further a career, is part of an arms-length relationship between an individual and an organisation. While the immediate feelings of 'terminated' employees may be as bruised as those of a European counterpart, there is no more rancour than in the case of a blue-collar worker who is laid off. It is accepted as the way things work. If the organisation's needs change again, those people may be hired back into the company at a later date. However, while a person belongs to an organisation he or she is expected to identify with its goals and to demonstrate dedication to it. Loyalties may be temporary but not less than whole-hearted.

Power in an American organisation resides with the Chief Executive Officer and is exercised through a small operating or executive committee of senior executives. Whatever other titles or position he or she may have the only one that matters is CEO. The board of directors, of whom several may be outside directors, is more like a German *Aufsichtsrat* than the British board of directors. The American board's main task is to appoint the CEO and it has little influence over day-to-day operations. The CEO's power and accountability is rarely shared. He or she appoints the executive committee and they are his delegates rather than his colleagues. There is much less feeling of collegiality than in a German or British corporation and little concept of shared responsibility. It is more akin to the French pattern. Vertical reporting lines are more important than peer relationships which tend to be intensely competitive.

Beneath the level of senior management, accountability is rigorously defined and meticulously reported, wherever possible in terms of profitability or some other financial yardstick. Americans are used to transparent organisations and are uneasy with the ambiguity and the hidden hierarchies that characterise many European companies. However closely organisational values are adapted to suit the indigenous culture of the host country the key disciplines of system and control are kept firmly in place.

Leadership

While the reality of American leadership style may not match up to the self-image of rugged, dominating individualism, at least not in the context of conformist business organisations, it is firmly based on the concept of individual accountability. The role of the boss is sometimes described as a 'coach', but in its sporting rather than its educational sense. Football and baseball coaches are considerably more directive than consultative. To carry the analogy further, coaches in American sport continue to manage and direct their players during the course of the game.

American bosses are not generally skilled or experienced in dealing with argument or open disagreement from their subordinates. They would tend to regard it as insubordination rather than constructive criticism. Conversely, it is sometimes hard for European superiors to evoke vigorous comment from American subordinates.

The outward egalitarianism of American manners is deceptive. Within a business organisation there is a well-defined and rigorously observed hierarchy. The position in the hierarchy has little to do with seniority or status or influence or any other 'social' determinant. It is determined by how much power you have. Power is measured in how much of the business is under your direct control. How this is evaluated varies from business to business — it may be the number of people reporting to you, the amount of profit generated, or the amount of earning assets.

Status is communicated by sophisticated titling systems, in which rank is coupled with function — Vice-President Finance, for example. Equally sophisticated is the salary and perks system that goes with it — the type of office, furniture, computer, country club membership, credit card, the quality of hotel you are entitled to stay in, eligibility to use the corporate jet and so on. Since company cars are not tax efficient and usually privately owned they do not feature in the status system.

Americans may lose patience with the participative, committee cultures of some countries. They do not look for consensus, in the sense of collective responsibilty for a decision jointly arrived at, but wholehearted commitment to a course of action for which one person carries total responsibility. Any vestigial notion of shared responsibility evaporates completely if it goes wrong.

Meetings are primarily a communication tool for imparting or gathering information, supported by the appropriate numbers or other hard facts. They are also the forum for the formal presentation of proposals for examination and ratification. An in-house presentation to a small group, or even one's boss, demands a professionalism more usually associated with a board presentation or a sales pitch in a European context. The object is not to make a decision — this will have been previously lobbied or subsequently approved — but to test the presenter's competence, preparation and depth of knowledge with sometimes trivial questions.

In dealing with colleagues at all levels it is important to demonstrate competence and professionalism. Bringing a problem to another, whether boss or subordinate or colleague, without a suggested solution and especially without all the relevant data, in the expectation that a solution will be worked out jointly, is a sign of weakness. Professionalism is demonstrated by a numerate, analytical approach to problem solving. Whatever the quality of the ultimate decision it will not have been made without exhaustive quantitative analysis. There is an antipathy towards unsubstantiated theory, qualitative as opposed to quantitative argument. This does not mean that decisions are necessarily more effective than more conceptual or intuitive decisions but they are ostensibly more rational.

It is also important to demonstrate 'aggression', which in the American sense means the dynamic pursuit of personal and corporate goals. The single-minded corporate and personal pursuit of profit is frank and unashamed. In more participative European cultures such self-motivation is sometimes interpreted as self-centredness. Conversely, Americans may find their European colleagues lacking in motivation and commitment.

Attitudes and behaviour

Etiquette

Many Americans are inhibited when first coming to Europe by a belief that social conventions are more formal than in fact they are. Similarly, many Europeans are misled by the apparent informality of American ways. Lurking beneath the relaxed and familiar style, the ready use of first names, the absence of ceremony, is a subtle code of manners that can be primly Victorian.

In the work environment day-to-day interaction is energetic and open. Business discussions may be forthright to the point of being brusque. Bluntness is preferred to subtlety. Some Europeans consider American openness as unseemly and brash, unaware that what they believe is their own sophisticated reserve may appear muddle-headed and devious.

At the same time, the essential assertiveness and competitiveness of business relationships is tempered by a greater degree of informal socialising and friendliness than many Europeans are used to. Monday mornings are for rerunning Sunday's ball game as well as the weekly staff meeting. Colleagues gossip about their family life and leisure activities to an extent that many Europeans would regard as intrusive. Meanwhile, Americans may find European reserve patronising and stand-offish.

Informality extends to the extensive use of humour on all formal and informal occasions. The joke is an obligatory warm-up to speeches and presentations. Humour can range from the hearty to the witty and the only taboo subjects are money or the company's products.

By no means all Americans transferred to Europe will work or expect others to work the long hours associated with certain industries or cities, notably New York. Generally speaking they prefer to start work earlier than Europeans and to go home to their families for an early dinner. But they will expect to be accessible at home in the evenings, at weekends and on vacation. The amount of vacation in Europe may come as a surprise. In the USA two or three weeks is the usual vacation entitlement and four is a maximum for senior people after long service.

Socialising

Business life extends deep into family and social life. Colleagues and their spouses are used to meeting regularly. Americans tend to stick together overseas not only because in many European countries there is no tradition of neighbourliness but because that is what they do at home.

Corporate status reaches outside immediate business circles. The importance given to business and the social status of businessmen is generally greater than in most European countries. An introduction to a stranger at a cocktail party often includes that person's employer and his or her title. Social standing is conferred by working for a prestigious company and diminished if that company's profitability takes a dive or bond rating slips. At social events business is often the main topic of discussion and despairing hosts may find the party split for the evening between those who go out to work and those who work with home and family.

JAPANESE IN EUROPE

In 1989 Japanese investment in Europe amounted to $30 billion. There are now about 400 Japanese manufacturing plants in Europe, of which 120 are in the UK. Although they employ no more than 100,000 people at present, Europeans may expect a wave of direct investment through the next decade. An increasing number of Europeans will have Japanese bosses, colleagues and business partners and the possibility of making a career in a Japanese company.

The indirect effect of Japanese management methods on European competitors and suppliers of Japanese companies is already pronounced. There is a growing school of management theory inspired by and imitative of Japanese models. While Japanese business culture in its entirety is outside the scope of this book, it is relevant to look at some of the ways in which it interacts with European business cultures.

From a European perspective there are two different aspects of Japanese management. One concerns the way that production and delivery processes are managed and the other is the way that individual colleagues relate to each other. The former 'hard' element of management is relatively easy to assimilate into a European context while the latter, the 'soft' element, is so unfamiliar that accommodation can often go no further than understanding and respect.

Two examples of hard management techniques that Japanese companies are instrumental in promoting are 'Just-In-Time' (JIT) and 'Total Quality' systems. The aim of JIT is to match, as nearly as possible, output with market demand in a continuous process beginning at the stage of long-range planning and ending when the product reaches the end user. The aim of Total Quality is to eliminate error and waste at all stages of the process. This is not just on the shop floor but at every level and in every activity of the organisation and every stage in the process.

As well as technical expertise, these systems demand above all a commitment of every person in the organisation to carrying them out. If they are perceived as yet another tool for management to control the workers then they fail. They will not work in a highly directive culture or one in which relations between different levels in the organisation are characterised by confrontation.

Planning, in every sense, including rigorous budgeting, is a vital part of the management process. Consistent with the stage of development of Japanese companies in the European market they take a long-term view. They tend to concentrate on sales and market share, not profit, and product development. Reporting on a few key variables is detailed and tightly controlled from the centre.

This approach is assimilable by Europeans because it is no less intrinsic to European business culture than to Japanese. The leap forward in Japanese quality from the shoddy mimicry of 50 years ago to today's pre-eminence was achieved to a great extent through the adoption and elaboration of primarily American scientific management techniques. Japanese re-introduce concepts which have been temporarily mislaid — craftsmanship, perfectionism, corporate pride, teamwork, cooperation. These are part of a European industrial tradition too and there is no reason to think that Japan monopolises them.

It is in the 'softer' areas, such as decision making, leadership and motivation, that the clash between the European and Japanese cultures is most tangible. It is sometimes stated, for example, that Japanese place a higher value on group norms, consensus and the acceptance of authority. But such a statement ignores much more fundamental differences in the underlying context of social relationships.

For a more thorough study of Japanese culture than there is scope for here, books like *Dealing with the Japanese* by Mark Zimmerman and *The Art of Japanese Management* by Richard Tanner Pascale and Anthony G Athos are well worth reading. What follows is based on conversations with British and American managers who have worked in Japanese companies in Europe.

Signals and symbols

To many westerners Japanese ways of thought and behaviour are pervaded with ambiguity, uncertainty and relativity. Europeans have to learn to interpret hints and subtleties and work with a greater degree of indirection and lack of clarity than they are used to. But this is a western perception. From the Japanese point of view their own behaviour is perfectly clear. They in turn find confusing and ambiguous many of the subtleties of speech and behaviour that Europeans take for granted. Westerners and Japanese do not share the same set of communication conventions. The meaning of body language, silence, manners, as well as language gets lost in translation.

For example, the conventions of listening are different. The western way of listening is to constantly impose judgement, to filter what we see and hear through a critical faculty. While listening, the Japanese engage in a practice called *aizuchi* — a series of 'yes' or 'I understand' like comments which serve to encourage the speaker. Westerners tend to make the mistake of interpreting aizuchi as agreement.

Independence versus interdependence

Western culture values the ultimate superiority of the individual over the group. In Japanese culture it is the opposite. Loyalty to one's immediate group is paramount and not even self-interest overrides the commitment to the welfare of the immediate community. This is a concept which westerners can accept in theory but whose everyday implications are sometimes difficult to cope with — interminable meetings, tortuous decision making, the sharing of responsibility — even for error, the duty to keep everyone in the group informed even about apparently trivial details. The idea of individuals sitting in their separate offices getting on with their work is an alien one for Japanese. Open plan offices are the norm even housing relatively senior people.

A Japanese organisation chart shows only collective units not individual titles and names. As a description of how the organisation actually works it is rarely more than an approximation. More important is the paternalistic social hierarchy and the complex network of personal relationships and obligations that weave through it. The hierarchy is based on seniority and experience, as much as responsibility, and reinforced by mutual obligations that go far deeper than the expedient loyalties of the West. Significant group relationships are not between peers, as they tend to be in the West, but between people of very different status and seniority. There is a mutually supportive relationship between a senior and a junior, more akin to the working relationship that a western manager would have with a secretary than with a subordinate.

This does not mean that a Japanese company is one big happy family, despite what its president, like his western counterpart, may claim. Individuals and groups compete strenuously and factionalism is rife. The difference is that individual success or failure is inextricable from that of the group. To westerners used to individual evaluation this can be frustrating. The corollary is that there is little personal recrimination for error unless that person has consciously overstepped the rules. His colleages get together and put it right. If there is a problem with that person it will be discussed within the group and if it cannot be solved the leader will be deputed to take it to a higher level. This is in contrast with the habitual western reaction to find someone to pin the blame on.

Harmony versus conflict

Western relationships are competitive rather than consensual. Winning is very important, whether it is a decision, an argument, or a genuine conflict. Competition is valued as creative and constructive. While Japanese are certainly not averse to winning they are even more averse to confrontation. Much of Japanese etiquette and behaviour, to western eyes rigidly conformist and irritatingly elusive, is designed to avoid any hint of conflict. Extreme politeness and deference, elliptical statements, vagueness, evasiveness and indecisiveness are disconcerting to westerners especially if they cannot read the real messages coming over. Likewise Japanese find western clarity, assertiveness, a love of debate and argument, divisive and embarrassing.

Westerners like to know where they stand. So do Japanese but not at the cost of disturbing the peace. Few westerners have not felt at some time like having it out with someone, getting things straight, putting things on the record, making their feelings known. They are disconcerted when Japanese colleagues, especially the boss, do not respond and side-step the issue, hoping it will go away. When faced with conflict among European subordinates they are often incapable of dealing with it.

Commitment and tenacity even to the point of obstinacy are prized in the west. To change your mind, to abandon a position without a struggle, are signs of weakness. Sticking to your guns in an argument, not letting go, even in trivial matters, indicates strength of character. To a Japanese it is the opposite. The ultimate 'he goes or I go' threat is incomprehensible to them.

Leadership

Westerners tend to value a tough, individualistic and dominating leadership style including the ability to take independent decisions and have them successfully implemented. The higher a Japanese manager rises in a company the more pains he will take to hide his ambition and capability and not to be seen as a forceful leader. Westerners who look for a decisive and charismatic boss are likely to be disappointed.

A Japanese manager concentrates on getting his group to work together. He is expected to be accessible, to work as an integral part of the group and to share whatever information he has. Because he has spent his whole career with the company, more often than not in the same type of function, he is expected to be fully knowledgeable about his subordinates' work as well as his own.

One of the problems Japanese managers often have with western subordinates is getting them to show initiative. They complain that Europeans need to be told what to do all the time. And when they have done it they need immediate assurance that they have done it right and a pat on the back. This would be embarassing to the boss and personally offensive to a Japanese subordinate who expects no more than a vague indication of the job to be done. Japanese do not have personal job descriptions or performance appraisal systems. Japanese job definition is for the group and it is assumed that everyone will do their best to fulfil it.

Their western subordinates on the other hand complain that they are given only vague hints of what they are supposed to do. Without defined responsibility, clear direction, and realistic goals they may find their jobs boring and without scope. When individual descriptions are instituted in Japanese companies in Europe it is usually at the European's insistence.

Europeans who discover the ground rules find that they have more scope to make their own jobs than in a circumscribed western environment. The ground rules are never do anything that is above your status, never do anything that infringes on someone else's status and never cut across hierarchical boundaries. The way to ensure you keep within the boundaries of your status is to keep your boss informed of the smallest detail. Among the sample of people I talked to it was those at the lower level of organisation who found this the most stimulating change from a European working environment where junior people are given comparatively little scope or responsibility.

Attitudes and behaviour

Etiquette

Japanese in Europe have reluctantly learned to use first names but feel more comfortable when addressed by the last name followed by *san*. Senior people may be addressed by their title plus san instead of last name. First names are reserved for family and close friends.

Titles, modes of address and language are carefully measured to indicate relative status, as are the other subtle status symbols of office life such as job titles or the positioning of desks in an open office. For example, seniors would have their backs to the windows where they could enjoy the privilege of natural light, in contrast with the fluorescent lighting pervading Japanese offices. While very sensitive to fine distinctions of rank, the western use of material goods to communicate achievement and authority are noticeably lacking. Offices are workmanlike, cars are unostentatious and so on.

More important than the actual forms of language and behaviour is pervasive politeness and a concern to avoid embarrassment to oneself or others. Displays of temper or any other uncontrolled emotions are seen as a sign of weakness.

Japanese manners are based on reciprocation, a sense of mutual indebtedness. To many westerners the excessive deference of a subordinate to a superior is less surprising than that it is returned in kind. Relationships between all levels are built on exchange, whether gifts, courtesies, help, information and so on.

Extreme politeness does not exclude openness in relationships. Europeans, especially women, may be surprised at the personal nature of conversations. This is usually because Japanese need to know people well before they can be comfortable with them. In some European countries you need not trust people to work with them as long as they do their job. In a Japanese environment there is a higher tolerance of professional and human frailty, but it is compensated with a greater demand for loyalty and trust.

Punctuality

Japanese are very punctual when politeness requires it and especially with senior people. Otherwise time is fluid. A meeting will carry on until it is finished or interrupted by the demands of a senior person outside. The working day can be very long, reflecting a demanding work ethic and a high level of commitment. Being the first to leave, even if you have no work to do, is a snub to the group and an embarrassment to your senior. As in Japan, Japanese may regularly work on Saturdays, rarely take more than a week's vacation or their full entitlement, and count sick days as holiday.

Humour

On informal occasions when they know everyone well, Japanese will be humorous and entertaining. At a formal meeting or among strangers they may be awkward and withdrawn and too nervous to loosen up. In presentations and speeches to westerners many have learned that the audience expects jokes and informality and respond accordingly. Japanese do not usually appreciate flippancy or triviality and find self-deprecation a mystery.

Social life

The most common complaint among westerners is that most major decisions seem to be made outside office hours by their Japanese colleagues. While in day-to-day activities they are kept well informed, they are kept in the dark about the overall direction of the company. For a westerner to progress in a Japanese managed company it is essential to work late in the evening and at weekends. This can be a major impediment for women who wish to progress in a Japanese company. In the workplace itself most of the women I talked to did not find Japanese more chauvinistic than their western counterparts. The difficulty was in establishing the appropriate relationships, as well as finding the time, to join in the after-hours discussions.

It is not so easy for men either. While the expatriate Japanese is considerably more flexible and adaptable to European ways than the stereotypical image of the chauvinistic and single minded Tokyo salaryman, it is hard to break into the inner circle. As in any foreign company a first requirement is to make an effort to speak the employer's language. As well as practically useful it demonstrates a commitment to career and company to which Japanese are particularly sensitive.

It is this level of dedication to the organisation which is probably the biggest hurdle to making any more than an averagely successful career in a Japanese company. The emotional and practical commitment that Japanese expect is incomprehensible to most westerners. The term 'British disease' is a byword among Japanese for idleness and is extended to most other western countries. The Japanese disease is *Karoshi*, or death by overwork. The difference between the British and Japanese diseases is perhaps the biggest cultural hurdle for each side to overcome.

THE WAY WE DO THINGS ROUND HERE

Some years ago I was hired by an American bank. I received a letter from the Head of Human Resources that started, 'Dear John, I am quite pleased that you have decided to join us.'

That 'quite' depressed me. I thought he was saying 'we're kinda pleased but I wish we had hired someone else.' Then I discovered that in American English 'quite' does not mean 'fairly', as it does in English English, but 'very'.

The first lesson is to learn the language. This was echoed again and again when I asked what foreigners should do to get on with their new colleagues. Even if your business partners speak perfect English it is worthwhile spending as much time as you can learning theirs.

The second lesson is not to jump to conclusions. If you feel offended or frustrated or even angry at something they have done or said you have probably misunderstood them.

Language is not just the words people speak. It is body language, dress, manners, etiquette, ideas, the things people do — their behaviour. And like language, behaviour has a grammar, an internal logic that is possible to understand and master.

Some of the differences may seem superficial — dress, etiquette, food, hours of work. Often it is simply a question of getting used to them, like the climate or the plumbing, while one gets on with the business.

Some of the differences, it is grudgingly admitted, may be an improvement. People are more courteous, service is better, you ask for something to be done and it happens without having to follow it up. Others can be irritating, like the conventions of punctuality. If you invite people to a party at 7 o'clock your guests will consider it polite to turn up on the dot in Germany, five minutes early in the American Midwest, an hour early in Japan, 15 minutes afterwards in the UK, up to an hour afterwards in Italy and some time in the evening in Greece. I deliberately avoided the more emotive word 'late' because there is nothing wrong in it. It is the accepted convention.

The problems begin when differences interfere with getting the job done. Delivery promises are not kept or suppliers are not flexible. There are no procedures or there are too many procedures. People never get together and thrash things out or meetings drag on all day. Decisions are postponed or they are taken without proper study. And so on.

When asked how he played evil men so convincingly, the actor Vincent Price replied that he did not play evil men. They did what seemed right to them at the time. The way others do things is not different out of stupidity or carelessness or incompetence or malice, although it may appear so. Most people do what seems the right thing to do at the time. The judgement of what is right is rooted in habit, tradition, beliefs, values, attitudes, accepted norms. In other words, the culture to which that person belongs.

An investigation into what lies at the heart of cultural differences leads into history, sociology, philosophy, theology, mythology, in fact every branch of the humanities. It is a fascinating study but outside the scope and length of this book which deals with how those underlying differences manifest themselves in people's day-to-day behaviour at work.

Culture is a woolly, flakey, pretentious, unbusinesslike, mildly derisive word like 'intellectual' or 'bureaucratic'. There have been attempts to find alternatives, such as climate or organisational ideology, but they are equally unsatisfactory. Culture has been defined in many ways, including the following:

A collective programming of the mind.

The sum total of all the beliefs, values and norms shared by a group of people.

The methods a society evolves to solve problems.

Everything we take for granted.

Patterned ways of thinking, feeling and reacting, acquired and transmitted mainly by symbols, constituting the distinctive achievements of human groups including their embodiment in artefacts; the essential core of culture consists of traditional ideas and especially their attached values. In many ways, culture could be described as the personality of society.

The definition of culture as it is used from this point on in the book is:

The way we do things round here.

ORGANISATION
AND LEADERSHIP

This book is based on a large number of anecdotes and impressions and judgements ranging from the trivial to the profound. Not that the trivial is unimportant. It can be a source of constant irritation as well as a focus for much deeper frustration. Etiquette may appear trivial — whether to use first names or last names, what to wear, how to behave at lunch or at meetings. But if you get stuck on this superficial level of interaction it is hard to penetrate to a more satisfying level of understanding and cooperation.

What seem to be superficial conventions of behaviour are often clues to more significant differences in the way people relate to each other and their work, punctuality for example, or when to wear a jacket.

Business issues like objectives or strategy or technology were rarely mentioned in conversations as areas of cultural difference. Difference of opinion yes, but not misunderstanding. Most of the difficulties occurred in the day-to-day interaction between bosses and subordinates, members of the same work group, other colleagues. By interaction I do not mean the degree of formality or friendliness or other aspects of personal relationship. I mean the way people relate to each other in a business context.

We are meeting to decide on an investment proposal. I put a lot of time into studying the reports before the meeting. It is evident that my British colleagues at the meeting are examining the papers for the first time. It wastes all our time. But it doesn't stop them giving their opinions.

Dutch engineer

My staff meetings are very annoying. It is very hard to get them to stick to the agenda. And they insist on discussing every point until everyone has had their say.

French manager of an Italian company

You have the impression that the French don't realise that they're at a meeting. They don't pay attention or they interrupt or they get up and make a phone call.

English director of a Franco–British company

So what determines how people interact? In what way does it differ from company to company and country to country? Two major factors predominate.

The first is a set of beliefs about an ORGANISATION and the role of the individual within it. How is work organised? How do you forecast and plan? How is information gathered and disseminated? How do you measure results?

The second is a set of beliefs about LEADERSHIP. Who has power? What is authority based on? Who takes the decisions?

There is a spectrum of belief in each of these dimensions which combine to influence how people behave towards each other.

There are many other dimensions and it is possible to break ORGANISATION and LEADERSHIP down into a number of elements. If the human brain were capable of assimilating them in a coherent picture I would do so. Like any oversimplified theory, and I have never come across a model of human behaviour that is not, it draws attention to what is omitted as much as what is included. It would be fatuous to claim that this, or any other model, is anything more than an aid to understanding. It is a working tool rather than an explanation. The most I would claim is that it captures a large proportion of the practical concerns and difficulties voiced by the people I talked to.

Organisation

This dimension is based on the extent to which it is believed that rational order should be imposed on human affairs.

At one end of the spectrum people believe that an organisation is like a machine, designed and built to certain specifications to achieve a precise objective. For the purposes of this book I have called this approach SYSTEMATIC. At the other end of the spectrum is the belief that an organisation is a social organism growing out of the needs and relationships of its members. I have called this ORGANIC.

You could also call the dimension MECHANISTIC-SOCIAL or TASK-PEOPLE or FORMAL-INFORMAL or whatever description you find most meaningful. They are all buzz-words whose meaning is loaded with bias, depending to which part of the spectrum you belong. What is important is to identify the ways of doing things that are associated with each end of the spectrum.

Systematic organisations

Towards the SYSTEMATIC end is the belief that the basic elements of organisation are functions which are coordinated by well-defined, logical relationships. The effectiveness of a systematic organisation depends on how well its functions have been designed to meet its goal. Relations between people are primarily determined by the function they carry out.

A SYSTEMATIC organisation exists independently from its members and its needs are more important than the needs of individuals. If there is a clash between order and the individual then it is accepted that order should prevail. Loyalty to the company prevails over loyalty to individuals.

What you do matters more than who you are. The relationship between the individual and the organisation is rational. It is based on a contract, explicit or implicit. There is a clear distinction between an individual's identity and his or her organisational function. The individual contributes skills to the organisation but is never absorbed by it. If what you do does not meet the needs of the organisation then you have no reason to belong to it.

165

Organic organisations

Towards the ORGANIC end of the dimension is the belief that organisations are like living organisms growing out of the needs of their members, their environment and the circumstances of the moment. Functions change, as do the relationships between them. There is order — otherwise there would be no organisation at all — but it is based on personal relationships and social hierarchy rather than a functional system.

The effectiveness of an ORGANIC organisation depends on how well its members work together to reach their common goal.

If there is a clash between order and the individual then the individual prevails or there is a compromise. This does not mean anarchy. It may mean that the order is re-examined.

The relationship between the individual and the organisation is blurred, not because it is irrational or emotive but because the distinction between them is not perceived. It is inconceivable that an organisation can exist independently of its members. It is not that who you are matters more than what you do — there is no distinction. Every member of an organisation has a part to play in it simply by virtue of belonging. Company loyalty means loyalty to individuals.

The extremes — anarchy and automatism

The ORGANIC end of the dimension can be extended to anarchism, where organisations, if they exist at all, are spontaneous and ephemeral. At the SYSTEMATIC end is auto-matism in which the organisation is seen purely in terms of functionality. Most European business organisations fall well within these two extremes.

Making assumptions visible

The assumptions people hold about the nature of organisations are for the most part invisible to those who hold them. They are more recognisable when translated into attitudes towards specific organisational processes.

The chart on pages 168 and 169 lists some of the attitudes of SYSTEMATIC and ORGANIC cultures. They are examples rather than an exhaustive list. As you skim through the list mentally tick off which statements you agree with most. It will give you an idea of where you come in the spectrum. The division will rarely be clear cut, but there will probably be a consistent bias.

Leadership

The LEADERSHIP dimension is based on the extent to which it is believed that power is given by groups to individuals.

This form of words was carefully chosen to reflect that a leader's authority, at least in a European business organisation, can only be exercised with the consent of the people who are being managed. The values associated with followership are identical to those associated with leadership.

The spectrum of belief about leadership ranges from INDIVIDUAL to GROUP. You could also call it the DIRECTIVE-PARTICIPATIVE, AUTOCRATIC-DEMOCRATIC, TOP DOWN-BOTTOM UP or AUTHORITARIAN-EGALITARIAN or whatever description you find the most meaningful. These words too are loaded with bias and ambiguity. What is important is to identify the attitudes and behaviours that are associated with different parts of the dimension.

Individual leadership

Towards the INDIVIDUAL end is the belief that individuals are intrinsically unequal and that the most effective or knowledge-able or competent take decisions on behalf of the others. Power is a right to be exercised by superiors over inferiors.

Group leadership

Towards the GROUP end of the dimension is the belief that while individuals may be unequal in ability and performance, everyone has a right to be heard and and to contribute to all the decisions that affect them. For the sake of convenience leaders are designated for as long as they embody the interests and the voice of those they represent.

The Organisation Dimension

ORGANIC	**SYSTEMATIC**

Forecasting

ORGANIC	SYSTEMATIC
Why bother? Who knows what will happen tomorrow?	Planning influences what happens tomorrow
Plans are based on hunches, intuition, experience	Plans are based on analysis
Plans are expressed in words	Plans are expressed in numbers
Opportunism is built in	Opportunities are identified
If the plan is not followed, change it	If the plan is not followed, enforce it

Decision Making

ORGANIC	SYSTEMATIC
Improvisation is valued	Nothing is left to chance
Decisions evolve	Decisions are made
Decisions are based on judgement	Decisions are based on facts
Ideas belong to their begetters	Ideas are independent
Procedures are traditional	Procedures are rational

Supervision

ORGANIC	SYSTEMATIC
Authority is based on trust	Authority is based on competence
Bosses should have personality	Bosses should have skills
Who you know matters most	What you know matters most
Authority resides in people	Authority resides in position
Power is delegated	Responsibility is delegated
Accountabilities are vague	Accountabilities are clear
People need inspiration	People want action plans

Control

ORGANIC	SYSTEMATIC
Errors are blamed on people and lead to recrimination	Errors are blamed on the system and lead to improvement
Criticism is personal	Criticism is objective
Only concrete numbers are trusted — e.g. sales or cashflow	Numbers are the only truth
Watch the people	Watch the results
People resent being monitored	People want feedback
Jobs are vaguely defined	Goals are precise

Communication

Communication is informal — the grapevine	Communication goes through official channels
People read between the lines — What does it mean?	People believe what is printed — what does it say?
The truth is never simple	Facts are clear

Reward

The right connections earn promotion	Competence earns promotion
Poor performers are transferred (up or down)	Poor performers are fired
Pay is related to seniority and status	Pay is related to performance
Success depends on luck	Success depends on skill
Educational qualifications indicate breeding	Educational qualifications indicate professionalism

Motivation

Honour calls	Duty calls
People strive for esteem	People strive for achievement
Personal feelings towards colleagues affect performance	Personal feelings have nothing to do with the job
People take pride in their status	People take pride in professionalism
Compete by outmanoeuvring	Compete by outperforming
You are right for the job or you are not	Skills can be taught

Style

Rules are to be circumvented	Rules are to be obeyed
Flair and creativity are valued	Reliability and thoroughness are valued
All is fair in business	Fairness is all
Titles describe your status	Titles describe your job
Informal associations and alliances are the real basis of the organisation	The organisation chart shows reality
Good old boys set the tone	Experts set the tone

The Leadership Dimension

GROUP	**INDIVIDUAL**

Forecasting

GROUP	INDIVIDUAL
Planning is done by those responsible for implementation, subject to minimal guidelines from the top	Planning is done by top management, and communicated downwards for implementation
Top management monitors only key financial results	Top management monitors every aspect of implementation
Everyone should know what the strategy is	Only a few people need to know what the strategy is

Decision Making

GROUP	INDIVIDUAL
Groups make decisions	Individuals make decisions
Consensus is paramount	Decisiveness is paramount
Decisions are made by those they affect	Decisions are made by designated decision makers
Decisions are passed down to be made by those who have to implement them	Decisions are passed up the line to those with authority to make them
Everybody's opinion counts for something	A superior's view always outweighs an inferior's
Individuals take initiatives if they will be accepted	Individuals take initiatives if they feel they can be imposed
Subordinates give agreement	Subordinates give information

Supervision

GROUP	INDIVIDUAL
Leaders fit the need of the moment	Leaders are born not made
Authority must be constantly earned	Authority must be demonstrated
Leaders stay close to their followers	Leaders keep their distance
Leaders are one of us	Leaders are a different sort
Leaders embody the will of the group	Leaders impose their will on the group
Leaders should be responsive and understanding	Leaders should be strong and tough

Leaders should have trust	Leaders should have charisma
Leaders look to their subordinates for support	Leaders coach and encourage their subordinates
Leaders persuade	Leaders instruct

Control

Quality is a mutual concern	Quality has to be enforced
Groups are accountable	Individuals are accountable
Informations systems serve those who do the job	Information systems serve those in charge

Communication

Communication is downwards, upwards and sideways	Communication is downward
There are no secrets	Information is shared on a 'need to know' basis
Meetings are for sharing information	Meetings are for briefing
Superiors can learn from inferiors	Superiors should know more than inferiors
People should be good listeners	People should be good communicators

Reward

Teams strive for goals	Individuals strive for achievement
Teams are rewarded	Individuals are rewarded

Motivation

Individuals work for the team	Individuals work for themselves
People are self motivating	People have to be directed
Harmony predominates	Competition predominates

Style

Hierarchy, status, titles are a convenience	Hierarchy, etc are essential
Modesty is prized	People should be assertive
Mutual support	Paternalism

The extremes — collectivism and absolutism

The GROUP end of the dimension can be extended to collectivist and the INDIVIDUAL end to absolutist. The collectivist belief is that power should be shared and exercised equally since all individuals are of equal value and take equal part and have equal weight in everything. The absolutist belief is that power is concentrated in the top person who acts as he or she sees fit whether other people like it or not. Most European business organisations fall between these two extremes.

Again it should be emphasised that these are attitudes shared by everybody in the organisation, not just the bosses. For example, an INDIVIDUAL leadership culture implies not only that bosses take decisions and give orders on their own responsibility but also that their subordinates expect them to do so and willingly execute the orders without question.

It is tempting to use the word 'democratic' in this context. Unfortunately it has several meanings, most of them emotive and loaded with bias. For example, a boss in an INDIVIDUAL leadership culture can go to great lengths to consult with subordinates about a decision. What he or she is looking for is information on which to base a judgement. The boss in a GROUP culture is looking not only for information but for participation in the responsibility for a decision. Both would regard themselves as 'democratic'.

It should also be remembered that the dimension deals with the role of individuals in the organisational process and not their personal style. It is possible to be unassuming and empathetic and still believe that you are the boss and the responsibility falls on your shoulders alone, just as it is possible to be macho and assertive and still believe that the only way to get things done is through the participation of a group.

The chart on pages 170 and 171 lists some of the attitudes associated with GROUP and INDIVIDUAL leadership cultures. Again they are examples rather than an exhaustive list.

CULTURE CLASH

By casting your eye horizontally along the charts on pages 168–9 and 170–1 you can get an idea of how the combination of ORGANISATION and LEADERSHIP dimensions can combine to create four very different cultural archetypes. To make discussion of them clearer in the following pages I have borrowed images from wild west mythology. (The company style is for alliteration not nationality).

INDIANS INC combines ORGANIC organisation with INDIVIDUAL leadership. It is led by a hereditary chief sanctioned by the spirits of the tribe. Organisation depends on tradition, precedent, folk memory and an intricate network of tribal relationships. Its logo is the totem pole.

CAVALRY CORP combines SYSTEMATIC organisation with INDIVIDUAL leadership. It is led by a commander who has worked his way up through an orderly system of ranks to a position of legally sanctioned and centralised authority. Organisation is based on procedures and manuals and a formal system of training and qualifications. Its logo is crossed swords on a flag.

POSSE plc combines SYSTEMATIC organisation with GROUP leadership. It is a well organised and legally sanctioned group of specialists with well defined targets. They elect a sheriff whose tenure depends on their support and his performance. He may appoint deputies among the group as long as they are willing to serve. Its logo is the sheriff's badge.

OUTLAWS SA combines ORGANIC organisation with GROUP leadership. It acts on collective authority, decision making and equal sharing of the spoils. Organisation is fluid, spontaneous, expedient and based on the personal relationships between the members acting as they see fit. A leader may emerge for the moment but is in danger of being shot in the back. They have no logo but wear various types of black hat.

If we put these cultural archetypes on a grid made up of the two dimensions — Leadership and Organisation — they look like this:

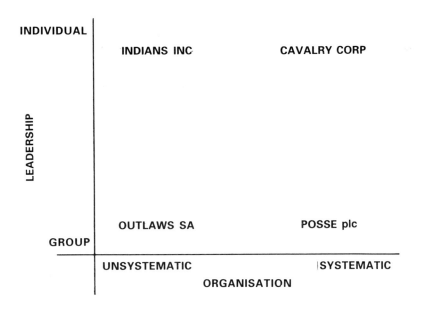

INDIANS INC

The INDIANS INC company combines ORGANIC Organisation with INDIVIDUAL leadership.

Take the example of forecasting. If it is done at all, it is the expression of a general strategy based on the experience, business sense and flair of the chief executive. He is prepared to change it if circumstances change. Only a few key people know what is in his mind, which gives him the opportunity of changing it without embarrassment and does not undermine his position if he gets it wrong. He does not have the tools to translate his plan into budgets and forecasts but concentrates instead on a few key indicators like sales or market share or cashflow.

CAVALRY CORP

The CAVALRY CORP company combines SYSTEMATIC organisation with INDIVIDUAL leadership.

Here, forecasting and planning are regarded as very important. They are still the preserve of senior management but are much more systematic. The chief executive has perhaps engaged a firm of strategy consultants, even if he does have his own strategic planning staff. When the plan is drawn up and approved by the board it is broken down into quarterly forecasts and monthly operating plans and presented to middle management. Adherence to the operating plan is closely monitored with a sophisticated pyramidal management information system culminating in the chief executive.

POSSE plc

The POSSE plc company combines SYSTEMATIC organisation with GROUP leadership.

The planning process is just as systematic as in CAVALRY CORP but many more people are involved. It starts at a low operating level with line management teams drafting their own plans and budgets during a series of planning conferences and meetings with their colleagues and staff advisers. Plans are centralised, consolidated, sent back for revision, redrafted and finally accepted. The sophisticated MIS system is designed to give the line manager as much feedback as possible.

OUTLAWS SA

The OUTLAWS SA company combines ORGANIC organisation with GROUP leadership.

There is probably no plan but everyone has their own idea of what it is. There are interminable discussions about where the company should be going and what it should be doing. Although there is no formal plan, so much debate and discussion about it leads to a consensus through the organisation of what the right direction should be. Attempts to formalise the consensus in a detailed forecast fail because people would not adhere to it and in any case the information and the techniques are not available.

Other examples of cultural difference

Culture is holistic. The following are a few more examples of the same underlying values and attitudes and beliefs which permeate every aspect of the way things are done.

Networking

In SYSTEMATIC organisations you cultivate those whose functions in the organisation overlap with yours. Competence and professionalism are more important than the quality of the personal relationship. In ORGANIC companies who you are matters more than what you do. Alliances are built up around trust and mutual obligation and may be based on coming from the same family, town, country, region, school, university, club, lodge, intake into the company or common work experience.

Teams

The concept of working in teams is common to most organisations. An organisation is in itself a team. But the team's structure and purpose and how its members interact is different according to the prevailing culture.

In a SYSTEMATIC culture a team is an assembly of specialists, each with a recognised contribution to make.

In an ORGANIC culture the composition and purpose of the team will be more loosely framed. Its members will see the goals of the team and their individual responsibilities as less clearly defined.

In GROUP leadership cultures teams — task forces, swat teams, project teams — can cut across hierarchical lines, a concept which may be permanently enshrined in the organisation with formal matrix management. This will be more difficult in INDIVIDUAL leadership cultures in which organisational clarity and reporting lines are given a high value.

Meetings

In SYSTEMATIC organisations there is a regular schedule of different sorts of meeting. Apart from regular briefing and information meetings there will be specialised task forces, committees and groups all with specified purpose and agendas and meticulous minutes. They start and end on time, even on the rare occasions when the business is not finished.

In ORGANIC organisations the distinction between a meeting and a get-together is much more blurred. They continue until all business is dealt with and if this is not possible, take up again at the next opportunity.

In INDIVIDUAL leadership cultures people complain about the number of meetings, however few there are. The senior person is in the chair and the point of the meeting is briefing, direction and information gathering.

In GROUP leadership cultures meetings are for sharing information, decisions, responsibility. They are taken seriously as an important tool for getting things done. There is a high value placed on listening skills. Consensus is the overriding goal.

Qualifications and training

Educational qualifications may be equally prized in all cultures but for different reasons. A SYSTEMATIC organisation is made up of experts, professionals and specialists. From an early age education tends to be vocational and technical. A high priority is placed on technical training at all levels of the organisation.

In ORGANIC cultures education indicates the sort of person you are, your social position. Experience and common sense, the University of Life, are seen as being of equal or greater value. Training, if there is any, is not prized for itself but as a privilege, an indication of status.

The diary

In SYSTEMATIC organisations, unless there is a real emergency, it is difficult to see anyone or arrange a meeting at short notice. Schedules and diaries are arranged long in advance, kept by secretaries and adhered to. It takes a lot of the stress out of life but also the excitement and the potential for creativity. In these organisations I was given an appointment days or weeks in advance and conducted my interview in a set time and left.

In ORGANIC organisations appointments are scheduled and rescheduled at short notice and the timetable is fluid. The diary is a guide known only to its holder — secretaries and assistants may not know anything about their bosses whereabouts. You can hold a meeting or get to see someone at short notice even if it means cancelling something less important. In really flexible cultures nothing will be cancelled and everyone will turn up at the same time.

To those from SYSTEMATIC cultures this sounds chaotic. But those who live within it are adept at managing the conventions to everyone's advantage. This book, for example, was much easier to research in such organisations. If it sounded interesting to the person I contacted, he or she saw me immediately, passed me on to others, invited me to sit in on meetings, and so on.

The litmus test

A litmus test for gauging where on the map an organisation lies is 'How important are meetings in getting things done? And do they start on time?'

The more important meetings are, the lower down the leadership scale the organisational culture is likely to be. The number of meetings or how long they take is not important. What is important is whether they are necessary in getting things done.

The more punctual people are, the more they will tend towards the SYSTEMATIC. People from the ORGANIC end of the dimension are not deliberately unpunctual. But sticking to a timetable is not an end in itself.

Transplants

Management styles or techniques or tools evolve to meet the needs of specific types of organisation. Theories about management are determined by the type of culture to which the researchers belong and in which the research was carried out. Because they work well in certain types of company they become fashionable, disseminated by consultants and academics and copied by organisations of widely different types.

Several things may happen to these grafts. They may succeed because they are suited to the new host culture. They may be rejected out of hand. They may be adapted by the culture out of all recognition. Or they may, in rare circumstances, change the culture itself. What is certain is that they will not survive independently from the way everything else is done in the organisation.

Take for example performance appraisal; in some companies it is laid down that at regular intervals, usually a year, employees meet with their bosses and discuss their performance. Both sides come to an agreement about the subordinate's job description, targets and standards of performance which are incorporated in a standard document. The appraisal is based on an objective review of these. The meeting with the boss is about what is necessary to improve performance — training for instance, or expansion of the job or getting promotion. The process is said to work best if it is disassociated from the pay review.

This is typical of a SYSTEMATIC-GROUP culture (POSSE plc). The underlying belief is that people take part in decisions that affect them, that they make the major contribution to their own performance, that it can be evaluated dispassionately and independently from their personal identity, that functions can be analysed and systematised, even that the appraisal process itself can be enshrined in forms and procedures.

But what happens when the CAVALRY CORP thinks it a good idea? The system remains the same — the forms are sent out by Human Resources and goals and targets are set and so on. But superiors and subordinates do not easily meet on common ground. To state blandly in the manual, that for the purposes of the annual appraisal interview, you should both sit on the same side of the desk and the boss should listen and ask questions and not impose his or her ideas, is unrealistic. Both sides expect the boss to give clear directions, to deliver judgements and encouragement and praise, to reward with payrises and promotion. It is an end-of-term report with grades and comments rather than a mechanism for sharing and negotiation.

In ORGANIC organisations it is difficult to set standards of performance because the underlying mechanisms do not exist. Performance is closely associated with personal qualities so that an objective discussion becomes embarrassing.

No single one of these four cultures is intrinsically superior to the others. Each of them is a product of its environment and the generally accepted values of its members. Decision making in POSSE plc is not necessarily superior or inferior to an entrepreneurial individual's flair in INDIANS INC. An organisation can be paralysed by rules and procedures or floundering because it has none. The position of the four hypothetical organisations on the map is no indication of their effectiveness.

But what happens when they get together?

MERGER MANIA

Let us imagine that each of our four companies have decided that they need to join forces with one of the others . . .

CAVALRY CORP and INDIANS INC

The first two to get together are CAVALRY CORP and INDIANS INC. They both have an INDIVIDUAL leadership culture but one is more SYSTEMATIC than the other.

It looks a good match. They are about the same size, have a complementary product range and are strong in different markets. Their chief executives hit it off on their first meeting. Each of them is a strong, forceful personality and control their companies with vision and a firm hand. Each of them secretly looks forward to the duel which will eventually result in one of them coming out on top. They eventually agree on a joint statement of intent.

When their professional advisers get to work there are some obstacles to overcome. CAVALRY CORP's lawyers prepare an agreement an inch thick while INDIANS INC's draft a one page letter of intent. The chief executive of INDIANS INC is happy to sign CAVALRY CORP's document as its essentials are in line with his letter and he can always renegotiate, he thinks, if circumstances change. CAVALRY CORP's boss is happy too as he had expected arduous negotiations on the fine print which ties INDIANS INC up in permanent knots.

CAVALRY CORP's accountants are less happy. They are

appalled by the state of INDIANS INC's books. Then they are shown, in confidence, INDIANS INC's real books. (The real real books are elsewhere.) CAVALRY CORP's accountants are also dubious about the complicated structure of shareholdings among INDIANS INC's shareholders and their relatives and friends.

Meanwhile INDIANS INC's accountants are appalled by what will be divulged. How can they continue to play their banks off against each other if everyone has the same information? And what about the tax authorities?

The marketing managers are having misgivings too. CAVALRY CORP is insisting on a swingeing rationalisation of the joint product range, concentration on a narrow market segment and reduction of the sales force. INDIANS INC's marketing manager thought the idea of the merger was to increase the product range and expand the customer base. They need to keep a foot in as many markets and with as many products as possible in case new opportunities open up. But he only has gut feeling to counter CAVALRY CORP's colour slides and printouts in fancy bindings with five year projections and simulations, market research, demographic charts and competitive studies.

CAVALRY CORP's marketing manager is nervous about associating himself with INDIANS INC's poor delivery and quality standards. He wonders how anything at all comes out of their apparently disorganised factory. INDIANS INC's manager is impressed by CAVALRY CORP's highly efficient and automated production line but nervous about their high prices and lack of responsiveness to design changes and individual customer requirements.

These differences over basic issues are compounded by growing friction in the day-to-day relationships between the managers. The biggest source of irritation for CAVALRY CORP's managers is INDIANS INC's inability to keep to deadlines. Information promised by a certain date arrives late. And when it does it is incomplete. They are never at meetings on time. They sometimes cancel them at the last minute or expect to set one up at the drop of a hat. And they never come properly prepared.

INDIANS INC's managers are irritated by CAVALRY CORP's

pedantic attention to detail. They want to do everything by the book. Meetings are frustrating because they never give enough time to the important issues. They often break off a discussion just as it is beginning to be interesting simply because they have another meeting to go to or a plane to catch. They are not very sociable either. Lunch is always rushed and unless there is a prearranged formal dinner they go straight home at the end of the day instead of going out for a drink and getting to know each other.

Eventually the chief executives break off the deal, both with relief. INDIANS INC would prefer a more flexible partner, CAVALRY CORP a more professional one.

INDIANS INC and OUTLAWS SA

INDIANS INC is approached by OUTLAWS SA. Although INDIANS INC is larger than OUTLAWS SA it looks a good fit. Both have an ORGANIC organisational culture but INDIANS INC has an INDIVIDUAL and OUTLAWS SA has a GROUP leadership culture.

More wary this time, INDIANS INC's chief executive enters into discussions. He is encouraged to find that OUTLAWS SA's approach to the market and their business philosophy and the way they are organised are very similar. INDIANS INC will be able to keep its identity and relative independence in OUTLAWS SA's loose and pragmatic organisation.

INDIANS INC's boss thinks he might do well out of it. OUTLAWS SA needs some strong leadership. The chief executive is not very impressive. For a start he has only one secretary and drives his own car. More important, he is indecisive and always looking over his shoulder at his deputy and his finance director. He will never commit to anything on his own authority.

Negotiations are fruitful but agonisingly slow. At least with CAVALRY CORP you could thrash things out with your opposite number. With OUTLAWS SA there are constant meetings and debates and discussions that include all sorts of people, some of whom have no apparent reponsibility in the area at all and some of them very junior. You think you have finally agreed something and on the next day more people make their appearance and it starts all over again. It is hard to pin down exactly who are the decision makers. And with so many people involved it is impossible to keep things confidential.

INDIANS INC's boss contains his impatience until a meeting in which someone from OUTLAWS SA says they could not go further until they were sure the workforce would go along with it. He gives them all a much needed lecture on the right of managers to manage.

Meanwhile OUTLAWS SA management is having misgivings too. INDIANS INC's managers seem more concerned with scoring points and establishing their position in the pecking order than with achieving a proper level of cooperation. OUTLAWS SA's people are not used to their assertive style at meetings and grumble about their arrogance.

OUTLAWS SA is also concerned that INDIANS INC will not fit into the management team. It is run like a personal fiefdom. All the decisions are passed up to the top and when he is not available the others will not take responsibility.

CAVALRY CORP and POSSE plc

Meanwhile CAVALRY CORP, having failed with INDIANS INC is having similar problems in his negotiations with POSSE plc. At first it is a relief, after INDIANS INC, to deal with people who are serious and professional. They are punctual and predictable and systematic. Quality permeates both companies.

But their negotiations drag on interminably. No-one in POSSE plc can make their mind up. CAVALRY CORP's organisation is streamlined so that no-one goes to more than two regular meetings a week, everyone knows what they have to do and gets on with it. But POSSE plc is bogged down in bureaucracy and time-wasting. You can never get hold of anyone, they are always at meetings. And, in CAVALRY CORP's view, the management of POSSE plc is at the beck and call of the unions. (Admittedly they have not had a strike in forty years.)

Meanwhile POSSE plc is having doubts about how exactly

their decentralised, divisional structure will be able to work with CAVALRY CORP's centralised, top-heavy organisation. Their operating units have little independent authority and refer everything back to head office . . .

This fiction illustrates the kind of culture clash that can arise when people of different organisational backgrounds try to work together. The greater the distance between them on the map, the more dramatic the collision. The worst case would be if INDIANS INC tried to work with POSSE plc. The only association likely to work would be an acquisition followed by the replacement of the acquired company's entire management.

Organisations do not have to go abroad to experience culture clash. The spread represented by our fictional companies exists in some form within every country in Europe. The size of the company, its recent growth, its industry, its region, all impact its culture. Small and medium sized family businesses will tend to be at the upper end of the leadership dimension, especially if they are still managed by their founders, as will traditional heavy industries such as engineering and steelmaking. Large companies and multinational subsidiaries will tend to be towards the SYSTEMATIC end of the organisation dimension. High tec companies tend to be SYSTEMATIC-GROUP while media and entertainment companies tend towards ORGANIC GROUP.

Differences within a given country or industrial sector tend to be along the organisation dimension. In many ways these are the easiest to fix. Imposing common standards of performance, reporting, budgeting, forecasting, planning, quality, systems, rules, procedures, codes of ethics, even punctuality and dress, is a question of education, communication or simple enforcement. These are the tangible elements of management. The elements on the organisation dimension are what business schools mainly teach. They are the subject of most books on business and the stuff of bread-and-butter training courses. They may not come naturally to people. At first they may be evaded, bureaucratised and manipulated, but constant usage and compliance and reinforcement will eventually create a systematic uniformity.

The leadership dimension encompasses mainly the intangible, people-oriented elements of management — leadership, followership, people skills. They are much harder to impose. These are the stuff of books and courses on such topics as leadership, team building, listening, presentation, assertiveness, conducting meetings, motivation. They are based on fundamental beliefs that individuals hold about themselves and other people. These beliefs are grounded much deeper than the technical aspects of management in the social, political and religious context in which people have been brought up. They are more likely to be uniformly held by those who share those backgrounds. And for the same reason they are much harder to change.

However much organisational cultures differ within a country the wider cultural background remains the same. There are common points of reference. It is when the organisations are seen against different national contexts that the differences between them are shown in sharp relief.

MULTICULTURAL ORGANISATION AND LEADERSHIP IN EUROPE

This is the bravest part of the book — putting the countries of the EC on the map. It would contain considerably more pages if every other statement were qualified with the warning that they were generalisations. But the generalisation represented by the MOLE Map is so enormous that it begs to be underlined.

Even the use of countries is suspect. There are arguments for using linguistic or racial or geographic regions instead of nation states — for example putting Northern France and Francophone Belgium together, while separating regions like Northern and Southern Italy.

The map looks only at business culture. It is tempting to toy with these ideas in the context of political systems, social structures and national character but these are outside the scope of this book. In most countries, the world of work is a sub-culture within a much larger context. When you go through the door of the office or the factory you enter a different sort of society from the one outside.

The MOLE Map

```
INDIVIDUAL
                    SPAIN           FRANCE

                                              USA
 L
 E
 A        PORTUGAL         BELGIUM            GERMANY
 D                                   LUX
 E
 R
 S
 H
 I                        IRELAND
 P
          GREECE              UK        DENMARK
              ITALY                  NETHERLANDS

     GROUP


     ORGANIC                              SYSTEMATIC
                      ORGANISATION
```

Reading the map

The relative position on the map of the various countries is more meaningful than their absolute position on the axes. Countries which are close together have such similar cultures that some companies within each may be interchangeable on the map. The further away from each other countries are, the more unlikely is this overlap. For example, the experience of working in a German, American or Danish company may be similar. But you are unlikely to find many German and Italian companies which are alike.

There are no absolute standards of behaviour. Somewhere in the world there are people who think Germans are messy and unpunctual. (The chances are they are in Switzerland). There are countries where Greece is regarded as a model of efficiency. There are countries in which French bosses would seem absurdly egalitarian and others where Italian company life would seem oppressively regulated.

> They are so inefficient. It is hard to get them to do things. At home I ask for something to be done, politely of course, and it gets done on time without any fuss. Here there are always problems, reasons why it can't be done the way I want it. If it gets done at all. Sometimes they just ignore me. You have to follow up much more here. Set deadlines. They always want to discuss things instead of doing them. Punctuality? Meetings never start on time. And they always drag on. You invite a customer to lunch at one o'clock and he arrives three quarters of an hour late and thinks nothing of it. It is very frustrating. I get very irritated and I don't know how to handle it.

Was this said by a Danish manager about working with British employees or by a British manager about working with Italians?

> They are so arrogant. They think that every meeting whether it's one-to-one or several people is a chance to show off, to dominate everyone else. They always try to score points. But as soon as the boss puts his foot down they hardly say anything. Except yes sir. There's rigid hierarchy, everyone in boxes. The boss takes all the decisions. Anything of importance gets passed up to him. He thinks he has to be right about everything.

Was this said by a Dutchman working with Germans or a German working with Frenchmen?

The answer to the two questions is 'both'. Danes and Germans think the British are inefficient and unpunctual while the British think the same about Italians and Greeks. Dutch think Germans are authoritarian and high handed and Germans think the same about the French. Our value judgements derive from perceptions about the ways others do things filtered through our own working practices and beliefs.

The attitudes that we express tend to be those which we would like to have or which reflect well on us. Many people believe they are more efficient and participative than they really are. The values that we incorporate in what we actually do may be different, like the man who spent an uninterrupted half hour telling me what a good listener he was. But however accurate self-perception is, almost everyone thinks that their way of doing things is the right way. We take pride in things that others may find incomprehensible or ludicrous or even immoral. The British are proud of what they call 'muddling through', Germans of what to others is obsessive thoroughness, Italians of compulsive improvisation. We find it hard to recognise the truth of criticism of the way we ourselves do things. If we do we try to explain away the criticism. Conversely the way others do things is thought inferior, even on the rare occasions when they are acknowledged to be more effective. Those on the right of the map may be heard to claim that those on the left of them are inefficient and disorganised and those on the right of them are cold and clinical and hairsplitting. They claim that those beneath them are indecisive and uncompetitive and those above them are domineering and egotistical.

Look again at the attitudes to Organisation on pages 168 and 169. They can all be rephrased as uncomplimentary negatives. If you are from a SYSTEMATIC culture you might regard the ORGANIC attitudes to decision making as based on snap decisions and gut feel and what worked well last time. If you are from an ORGANIC culture you might see SYSTEMATIC decision making as unimaginative, overconservative and hidebound by procedures and overanalysis.

E is for Europe

The map describes primarily European cultural differences. The USA is included because American business culture originally derives from European and has returned the favour in the past fifty years. It is not so useful when looking at, for example, oriental business cultures, which is why Japan is left out. Why? Because there are other dimensions which are equally if not more important than Organisation and Leadership. In Europe these factors can be ignored for practical purposes because we all share the same beliefs about them. And shared beliefs tend to be invisible.

For example, it is a basic assumption of the MOLE Map that the basic unit of reference is the individual person. The dimensions examine the individual's relationships (a) with other individuals and (b) with the elements of organisation. From our western point of view this seems completely normal but may not be so relevant in oriental or African cultures.

> You have to understand that we are a nation of individualists.

This was said in almost every conversation, irrespective of nationality. We believe that we are individualists in the same way we believe we are efficent and honest. Individualism is at the heart of western culture. (Even such a basic concept should be treated with care as it can mean different things in different national contexts. In the UK it means non-conformity, in the USA self-reliance, in Latin countries self-centredness, in Germany autonomy.)

In whatever sense it is used individualism has no correlation with beliefs about leadership and co-operation. Individualism may be given as an explanation for directive authority needed to keep people in line or for collaborative mechanisms designed to reconcile independent individuals. Those from INDIVIDUAL leadership cultures may consider GROUP leadership conformist while those from GROUP leadership cultures consider INDIVIDUAL leadership subservient.

MULTICULTURAL MEETINGS

Recognising cultural difference may be helpful in avoiding misunderstanding between individuals. But how can it be used constructively?

The range of situations in which readers may come across culture clash is vast, ranging from an annual visit to a trade fair to implementing a multinational merger. As a practical example of a culture-sensitive approach in a frequent situation let us take a monthly coordination meeting between representatives of companies from different countries involved in some kind of association.

Let us also assume that each of them is a stereotypical example of their national culture. How can we predict from the MOLE Map, and the other generalisations in this book, how they might behave? And what can be done to make their meeting as productive as possible?

Language

The first problem is language. It is most likely to be English, which will suit the North Europeans, or French, which may suit the South Europeans more. Whichever is chosen, there will be some participants who feel at a disadvantage because they do not speak it as fluently as others at the meeting. There is a risk that linguists will dominate the less fluent.

The language problem should be brought into the open by making the working language or languages the first item of discussion. It may be advisable to make arrangements for preparatory papers and minutes to be translated. At the meeting itself it may be decided that people may speak in any language they choose which is comprehensible to the rest. Some members may wish to bring along to the meeting 'chuchoteurs' or 'whisperers', in other words personal simultaneous translators. Whatever is decided, the rules should be made clear.

Expectations

Participants will have different expectations of the function and outcome of the meeting. For those towards the INDIVIDUAL end of the LEADERSHIP dimension — French, Belgians, Spanish, Portuguese, Germans — the purpose will be to brief the others with information. If it is clear that the meeting has to result in an agreement or a joint proposal, they will come armed with a detailed plan which they will attempt to impose on the others with as little amendment as possible.

Those towards the Group end — Dutch, Danes, British, Italians, Greeks, Irish — will expect the meeting to pool information or problems and take steps to resolve them on a basis of consensus and compromise. If they have developed a plan of their own, it will be a working hypothesis to be negotiated and amended, rather than a position to be defended.

For those at the ORGANIC end of the ORGANISATION dimension — Italians, Greeks, Spanish — informal networking in the bar or over coffee or during lunch is as important as what goes on at the meeting itself. The meeting will give a formal sanction to what has been discussed or agreed outside. For those at the SYSTEMATIC end the extra-curricular socialising, while it oils the wheels, counts a lot less than what goes on at the meeting itself.

Time might, therefore, be allocated to both formal and informal socialising. Arrange to meet for dinner the night before. If there are French or Spanish participants allow two hours for a proper lunch. For some participants this will be the most constructive part of the event.

Preparation

Those towards the SYSTEMATIC end of the ORGANISATION dimension — Germans, Dutch, Danes — will be well prepared. They will expect briefing papers which they will study and amend and whose implications they will have meticulously researched. Those towards the ORGANIC end — British, Italians, Spanish, Irish, Greek — will have skimmed through the papers on the plane, and some may still be leafing through them at the meeting. They expect that what is actually said at the meeting has more importance than what is written in the briefing.

The chair should ensure that working papers are distributed well in advance with a request for comments on them before the meeting, to check that each participant has received them and, preferably, read them.

Attendance

The further towards the ORGANIC end of the ORGANISATION dimension — Italians, Greeks — the more unpredictable it is who and how many will turn up, regardless of who has been designated.

If the designated participant cannot attend those towards the GROUP end of the LEADERSHIP dimension — British, Dutch, Danes — will send a subordinate who may be much more junior. Higher up the dimension they will either send an immediate and trusted deputy or no-one at all. Unaccustomed to meetings between people of different status they will ignore the deputies of others.

Punctuality

Everyone will try to be there on time, but only those at the SYSTEMATIC end of the ORGANISATION dimension can be relied upon to succeed. They will expect the meeting to start and end on time even if the aims of the meeting have not been fully achieved. If the meeting is called half an hour before the formal proceedings start it gives time for the unpunctual to arrive and for the others to socialise over tea and coffee.

Some participants, probably French or Italian, may feel less bound by the discipline of a meeting than others. They may leave to make phone calls or attend to paperwork if the discussion is not immediately relevant to them. One solution is not to serve refreshments during the meeting and to schedule interruption by breaking every hour for refreshment, small talk, telephone calls and other personal business.

Be over generous with time. Add at least half an hour on to the end of the projected schedule for slippage. Punctual people do not mind leaving early.

Agenda

Everyone will expect a prepared agenda but only towards the SYSTEMATIC end will they expect to keep to it. The moderately ORGANIC, like the British, will expect to discuss and amend the agenda at the beginning of the meeting while the more ORGANIC will feel free to introduce unscheduled topics at any time.

If possible agree the agenda with each participant before the meeting and again at the start. Make the individual items as specific as possible, including the desired outcome of the discussion and the time allocated for it.

Chair

Those at the INDIVIDUAL end of the LEADERSHIP spectrum — French, Belgians, Spanish — will expect strong control from the chair over the agenda and the discussion. They will also find it natural to contradict and challenge the chair and vie for the real authority, as distinct from the formal, over the proceedings. Others will expect the chair to be more unobtrusive but his or her position to be more respected.

At the SYSTEMATIC end participants will expect contributions to be made through the chair when invited. At the ORGANIC end they will expect more of a free-for-all and feel less constrained by formalities of debate.

If possible it should be agreed before the meeting who will chair it, whether the chair rotates and so on. The chair should make clear whether discussion will always be through the chair or not. At first it is as well to make participation as formal as is necessary to ensure both orderly progression through the agenda and the contribution of every participant.

Participation

Participation will have different styles of contribution depending as much on their individual personalities as on their nationality. The following are extremely stereotypical and are examples of different styles that any participant could adopt.

German style is to be well-prepared and to contribute only when they feel well qualified to do so and when they have something useful to say. They will not expect to be interrupted or immediately contradicted and regard their prepared positions as incontrovertible.

French contributions tend to be adversarial, dogmatic, and models of rationality. They expect their own and others' contributions to fit in to an overall schema or theory. They expect to be contradicted and to win the argument by logic and assertion.

Italian contributions tend to be innovative, complex, creative and usually stimulating. They are embellished with definitions, caveats, analogies allusions and asides, and in the opinion of the rigorously pragmatic not always relevant.

British contributions tend to be pragmatic and realistic. They may not always be supported with hard fact, offering opinion and assertion for discussion rather than proposals for adoption or imposition. Their predeliction for humour may relieve tense or tedious moments but it can also be regarded as trivialising. They are the least likely to lose interest or temper.

The Dutch have a similar approach to the British in terms of seeking a common resolution instead of imposing one, preferring the practical to the theoretical and in using humour to defuse conflict and tedium. Their contribution will be brutally frank.

Spanish tend not to risk embarrassment or discomfiture by saying anything that might be criticised for any reason ranging from a poor command of the language spoken to the actual content. This can be mistaken for aloofness. They will participate in emphatic and spirited debate as long as they feel on firm ground.

Consensus

There is a difference between passive concensus, meaning that the participants consent to a course of action, and active consensus meaning that they are fully committed to it. Those towards the ORGANIC end of the ORGANISATION dimension may give their assent to a decision but will not abide by it. Those towards the SYSTEMATIC end will only assent to what they feel committed to carrying out.

Those towards the GROUP end of the LEADERSHIP dimension will look for a genuine consensus based on a synthesis of views. Those towards the INDIVIDUAL end will seek consensus based on the adoption of the best idea, preferably their own.

The depth of agreement primarily depends, of course, not on cultural difference but on the underlying business interests that each of the participants represent and how much authority they have to commit them. This may not always be clear. In any event it is wise to aim for complete and active consensus. Majority decisions should be avoided and formal voting postponed until the very last. Consensus oriented participants should be prepared for apparently irreconcilable positions to be hotly contested by the others before coming together quickly at the end.

Follow-up

Those towards the SYSTEMATIC end will expect the meeting to have a definable result and a commitment to concrete actions, steps to which everyone is committed and for which responsibilities have been allocated. The more ORGANIC will regard the less tangible results of the meeting — mutual understanding, a reaffirmation of the will to cooperate, a sense of where the venture is going, as more important than specific steps.

As far as possible the form of the desired outcome should be agreed beforehand. However, it should not be assumed they will be adhered to by everyone without being chased up afterwards.

POSTSCRIPT

No culture is static. Some are changing faster than others but they are all in transition towards a homogeneous European business culture. Information technology, international competition, influence of multinationals, education, economic deregulation and, increasingly, the single market are pushing companies in all countries to the SYSTEMATIC end of the organisation dimension. At the same time companies at the INDIVIDUAL end of the leadership scale are becoming more aware of the need to share responsibility and power more evenly throughout the organisation in the interests of quality, productivity and innovation.

The most active agents of change are senior managers and young professionals. The education and expectations of young people lead them to demand a different management and organisational style. Among senior managers, the national stereotypes are rapidly giving way to a breed of internationally oriented, professional managers. These are mainly to be found in larger companies. Among those who kindly read drafts of the chapters of this book relating to their country of operation a frequent comment was 'yes, that was the old way of doing things but things are changing'. Their position as individuals on the MOLE Map may appear much closer to each other than that of their countries of origin.

I embarked on this project with considerable scepticism about national stereotypes. It was surprising therefore to discover how consistent observations were from people of different nationality, age, sex and background. Whether or not they exist in reality, stereotypes certainly exist in the perception of outsiders. And it is in perceptions of behaviour that misunderstandings occur. Avoiding them will make collaboration not necessarily more harmonious but at least more productive. And that, after all, is the test of the Single Market.